HIS FINAL GIFT

HIS FINAL GIFT

25 LESSONS FOR FATHERS

Jamie Dewald

ISBN-13: 9781518645815
ISBN-10: 151864581X
Library of Congress Control Number: 2015917266
CreateSpace Independent Publishing Platform
North Charleston, South Carolina

This book is dedicated to my beautiful wife, Liza, and my two sons, Micah and Jonah. God, in His infinite grace and mercy, has chosen to bless me with an amazing family. Thank you for loving, encouraging, and supporting me.

TABLE OF CONTENTS

Although this book was written specifically for fathers with sons, there is no doubt that the information and lessons in this story are equally beneficial to fathers with daughters, as well as to mothers. Most of the timeless lessons in this book are taken directly from the Bible, the ultimate life instruction book. I sincerely hope that it adds value to your life.

A WORD FROM THE AUTHOR:

Luke 2:39-40
*"When Joseph and Mary had done everything required by the Law of the
Lord, they returned to Galilee to their own town of Nazareth. And the child
(Jesus) grew and became strong; he was filled with wisdom, and the grace
of God was upon him."*

THIS IS ONE of the foundational Scriptures upon which this book was written. In fact, I think it would do all parents well to have this passage as a
cornerstone of their family values. It's easy sometimes to read the Bible
and automatically discount what is being taught because we can't relate
to it. We think things like, "Well of course Mary was a great mother. She
was hand-picked by God to raise the Savior of the world." Or, "This verse
is talking about Jesus. He is the Son of God, so of course raising him is
different than raising my child."

I certainly understand that line of logic, but let's simply take this passage and apply it to mothers, fathers, and children today.

"When Joseph and Mary had done everything required by the Law of the Lord…"
I believe that all Christian parents should ultimately have two main
goals: 1) To raise their children according the truth of God's Word.
2) To raise their children to become godly young men and women. If
they accomplish this then they have certainly *"done everything required by
the Law of the Lord"* as it relates to parenting.

"And the child grew and became strong…"

One of our tasks as parents is to help our children to become strong spiritually, physically, emotionally, and mentally.

"he was filled with wisdom…"

Knowledge, education, and experiences are all of great value, but none compared to instilling wisdom in our children.

"and the grace of God was upon him."

What could possibly be better than knowing that the grace of God is upon our children? That God has created, chosen, called, sanctified, and made His grace and mercy available to our children. Why? For His glory; for His purpose; and for His kingdom.

As you read this book, please do so with this passage on your heart and mind.

Jamie

CHAPTER 1

THE LAST CALL

IT WAS 12:45 p.m. on Sunday as David and Hailey Williams pulled into their driveway. They had just returned home from a powerful worship service at church. Hailey was in her typical joyful, fun-loving mood. As she was always smiling and laughing, David was often amazed at how she was happy and positive no matter what. He would jokingly tell his friends, "She's married to me! Can you blame her for being happy all of the time?" David adored everything about Hailey, but her joyful personality was probably his favorite characteristic.

David Williams is a thirty-one-year-old student minister. His amazing wife Hailey was eight months pregnant with their first son, Noah. They lived in Louisville, KY, but they were both originally from Atlanta, GA. They met at a college Bible study and immediately hit it off. David was attracted to Hailey's bright smile and cute laugh. And it didn't hurt that she was a knockout! Hailey always told David that she was attracted to his sense of humor, outgoing personality, and kind spirit. Even though this Bible study was simply a bunch of college kids who got together each week to study and pray, it was obvious to her that David was clearly the leader of the group. He always took charge, but not in a negative, domineering way. Hailey had told David a number of times about the time she called her mom to talk about this new, great guy she met. "He is such a servant leader," she told her mom. "I really like him."

David and Hailey quickly fell in love and got married right after college. Although neither one of them had ever lived anywhere other than Atlanta, they immediately packed up and moved to Louisville, KY. David felt a strong calling to ministry, so he enrolled in seminary and they began their new lives together, young, broke, and in love.

Although they had not planned on staying in Louisville after semi-nary, David got a great job as a student minister with an amazing church. David loved his job and Hailey loved the people in the church, so they planted their flag and decided to make a life in Louisville. They tried to get pregnant, but Hailey had some complications. They tried everything they could think of, but nothing seemed to work. It was a hard time for Hailey. She wanted to be a mom more than anything else in the world. But after several years of fervent prayer, Hailey finally got pregnant.

"Honey, you go get changed, and I will start fixing lunch," Hailey said as they walked in the door from church.

"Baby, you look like you have a beach ball in your stomach," David said jokingly. "Kick your little feet up and I'll make lunch."

"The only thing you know how make is cereal and sandwiches," Hailey joked back.

"Sandwiches it is!" David said with a smile.

"Well, you better hurry. The football game starts in ten minutes," Hailey added.

David was a passionate Denver Broncos fan. He loved watching quar-terback Peyton Manning, and he almost never missed a game. Although she didn't care too much for football, Hailey usually sat with him and watched the games. David knew that she didn't like football, but he loved that she tried. After all, it gave him someone to complain to whenever the Broncos were losing.

As the clock of the football game clicked down to halftime, David looked over at Hailey. He was in a great mood because the Broncos were winning by fourteen points.

"Peyton is in the zone today!" David said with enthusiasm.

"What?" Hailey said, looking up. "Are we winning? What's the score?"

David started laughing as he quickly realized that Hailey was not quite as excited about the game as he was. In fact, she had zoned out a long time ago. She had her shirt lifted up and was rubbing her belly.

David came back to reality. When he watched football, it was like he went into another world. Hailey had learned early in their marriage that having a serious conversation during a football game was a bad idea.

"Do you want to feel him kick?" said Hailey while rubbing her belly.

"Absolutely!" David said as he muted the TV and walked over to the sofa that she was lying on.

Hailey grabbed his hand and placed it on her belly. "Put your hand right here and be still," she said.

After a few seconds, David felt a kick and started laughing.

"Keep your hand there. He's moving a lot right now," she said.

With his hand still there, David lowered his face to her belly. "Noah! Noah can you hear me? It's Daddy. Can you move for me, little buddy?"

As baby Noah continued to move around, David and Hailey just smiled and laughed. After a few minutes of enjoying this show that Noah was putting on, Hailey broke the silence. "Can you believe he will be here in a month?"

"I don't know if I am more excited or more nervous," David said with a serious look on his face.

"Nervous?" Hailey asked. "Why would you be nervous? This is the most exciting time of our lives."

"You're right, honey," David said as he quickly changed his tone. "I am excited. I truly can't wait. I guess I just want to make sure that I am the best dad to Noah that I can be."

Hailey leaned up and gave David a kiss. "You are going to be a great father. I know it."

"Thanks, baby. I love you," David said with a smile. But deep down he was scared to death. He had no idea how to be a father. Over the last few months, Hailey had probably read a dozen books on pregnancy and parenting. David briefly skimmed through some of the parenting books, but he felt that they were mostly geared toward mothers. Even though he was thirty-one, most of his friends were either still single, or married but with no kids. David had very little experience with children. He was usually a very confident guy. Not arrogant, but he carried himself with confidence. He either knew what to do, or he figured it out quickly. But when it came to being a dad, David was clueless. He wanted so badly to be a great father; he just didn't know what to do.

"The game is back on," Hailey said as she pointed to the muted screen.

"Oh, thanks, honey," David said. He was so deep in thought that he didn't realize that he had already missed a few minutes of the second half. He gave Hailey's belly one final kiss and then returned to the game.

At 8:07 p.m. the phone rang. David didn't even look to see who it was.

"You're late!" David said with a smile on his face.

It was his father, Tom Williams. Tom called his son every Sunday night at exactly 8:00 p.m. without exception. In fact, Tom was so precise with this weekly ritual that it had become a running joke if he was even a couple of minutes late. Tom began calling David every week when he was in college. David recalled the morning he left for college, his dad hugged him and said, "I'll check in on you each week. I'll miss you son. If you ever need to talk, I'm here."

In fact, David couldn't remember a single time when his dad had missed a week. When David was in his early twenties there were times when he would get annoyed and not even answer the phone. Sometimes he would be in a hurry and say something like, "Dad, I'm sorry, but I'm very busy right now. Can we talk next week?"

Tom never got frustrated, and he never called back if David didn't answer. As David got older and experienced more of life, he came to relish his phone calls with his dad. In fact, it was one of his favorite times of the week. David and Tom had always been very close. David was an only child, and so his dad became his best friend. He could talk to him, not only as a father, but also as a friend. As a student minister, it was so valuable for David to have someone to talk to. He didn't have to be *pastoral*, and he didn't have to be *on* all of the time. He could just be himself. He could be real, no matter what.

Tom was a wealth of wisdom. Any time David had a problem or issue, he called his dad. Tom always seemed to give good, practical advice. David often wondered how he knew so much.

"Sorry I'm late, son. I guess the streak is over. You'll never let me live this down, will you?"

"Seven minutes late! I was beginning to worry. I had just told Hailey that something most have happened," David said with a smirk.

"I know it. I was working in the garage, and I lost track of time. I've let that place get a bit too messy, so I needed to clean it up. I would still be in there if your mom hadn't yelled at me," Tom said.

"Working in the garage?" David said, trying to not sound so parental. "Dad, you know the doctors told you to take it easy. Please don't overdo it."

Tom started laughing. "Have you been talking to your mom? You two sound the same."

A year and half ago, Tom had been diagnosed with brain cancer. To say that everyone was shocked and surprised would be an understatement. Tom was very active and healthy. He ate clean and worked out regularly. David often told him that he was more physically fit in his fifties than most of his friends in their twenties were. Tom always pumped himself full of vitamins, fruits, and vegetables, and he was almost never sick.

One day after dealing with an intense headache and dizziness, Tom's wife Ann finally convinced him to go to the doctor. They were expecting to get some over-the-counter medicine. But what they got instead was news that changed their lives. Tom had a large mass in his brain. After many tests, it was discovered that he had a golf ball–size tumor in his brain. It was malignant.

Tom, being the eternal optimist, insisted that everything was OK and that he should get a second opinion. Another doctor confirmed what Ann had feared. This cancer would take his life. It was too deep in the brain to operate, and too large to kill. The first doctor gave him three to six months to live. The second doctor said he might live one year if he was lucky. Both doctors recommended chemotherapy treatment and radiation, but Tom refused. One Sunday night when David asked him to reconsider the treatment, Tom said, "The cancer may kill me, but I'm not letting those chemicals take me out. If I go down, I want to go down mentally and physically strong."

Tom had already lived over a year beyond what his first doctor predicted, and six months later than the second. He still worked out each week, led a weekly Bible study, and volunteered often. He had good days and bad days. Some days he would suffer from migraines and dizziness, and some days he was nauseous and sick. But Tom never complained. If you saw him around town or at church and asked how he was doing, he would always give is famous catchphrase: "I'm just living the dream!"

David knew it was a losing battle to try to convince his dad to slow down, so he tried a different approach. "How are you feeling this week, Dad? And don't say that you're living the dream. I know you are. But really, how are you?"

"David, I feel great," Tom said with an appreciative tone to his voice. "Some days are rough, but I'm thankful for the good ones. And today is a good one."

"That's great to hear, Dad. You are the strongest man I know," David said.

Tom smiled and said, "I appreciate that, buddy. We really are blessed, you know that, David?"

"Yes, sir," he said.

"I have been thinking about this a lot lately. For some crazy reason, God has chosen to bless me with an incredible life. He gave me the most amazing woman in the world and somehow convinced her to love me these past thirty-five years," Tom said.

"Yeah, I don't know what she was thinking," David added. He was trying to be funny so that he didn't start crying.

"I ask her that every day," Tom joked as he continued. "But seriously, son, I am blessed. God, in his generosity, has given me the most amazing son and daughter-in-law. And now to have little Noah almost here! It doesn't get any better than this, David. If Jesus decides to bring me home soon, I'm ready. Think about it, David. If God leaves me here, then I get your mom, you, Hailey, and Noah. If God takes me to heaven, then I get Jesus. It's a win-win!"

David couldn't talk. He was fighting back tears. He always tried to be strong and positive because he knew how important it was to his dad. But he was starting to lose it. His dad was his mentor and hero, and he was losing him. This had been a really hard time for David.

After a few seconds of silence, Tom could sense that David was trying hard to not cry. So he decided to lighten it up and change the subject, so he said, "Enough about me, David. How's my girl doing this week?"

David swallowed the knot in his throat and said, "Hailey is doing great. I told her today that she looks like she has a beach ball in her belly. But she didn't think it was as funny as I did. Actually she is getting around really well. We went to church this morning. As long as she stays active, she's fine. But when she sits for a while, her ankles swell and her back hurts. But that just gives me something to rub, right? At least that's what she keeps telling me."

"Hey, you give my sweet girl whatever she wants," Tom exclaimed. "What about Noah? How many more days is it now?"

David answered, "Only four more weeks. Can you believe it? He's almost here. He was kicking like crazy today. I think he's ready to come out. Either that or he was cheering with me during the Broncos game."

"Your mom and I can't wait to see you guys," Tom concluded.

When David and Hailey moved from Atlanta to Louisville, it meant that they got to see their family only a few times a year. But since Noah was soon to be the first grandchild in the family, Tom and Ann were even more eager to see them.

"The C-section is still scheduled for 8:00 a.m., right?" Tom asked.

"Yes, sir," David answered.

Tom started to say good-bye. "I'm praying for Hailey and Noah every day. Have a great week, son."

But David interrupted, "Hey, Dad, before you go, can I ask you a question?"

"Of course," Tom quickly answered.

"Before I was born, were you nervous about being a father?" David asked sheepishly.

"Nervous! Are you kidding me? I was scared to death," Tom replied with laughter. "I think all dads get scared. Parenting seems to come natural to mothers. They start thinking about babies when they are little girls. I think God made women special that way. But men really have to work at it."

David sighed. "I'm so glad to hear you say that. I'm a nervous wreck. But you were truly the best father I've ever seen. How did you do it? Like you were just saying, it's definitely not natural for me. But I want more than anything to be a great father, like you."

As Tom was about to respond, David interrupted, "I'm sorry, Dad. Hailey is yelling for me. She needs my help."

"That's OK, son, you go take care of her," Tom said with a quiet confidence. "We can talk more next week. I would love to pick up where we left off. Actually, I have something that I want to give you."

"What is it?" David asked with curiosity.

"It can wait," Tom said quickly. "Now's not the time. Have a great week. I'll talk to you next Sunday. I won't be late next time."

"I know you won't, Dad," David said with a smile.

"David, always remember three things," Tom said with enthusiasm. "Number one, you are special. Number two, God loves you. And number three, your dad loves you."

David had heard these words a thousand times. Ever since he was a young child, his dad would say this to him every night at bedtime. When he was a teenager, he asked his dad to stop saying it. But he never stopped. Even when David went off to college, these were the last words his dad said to him. And of course, through the years each Sunday night, he would end their phone conversation with these same three statements. David loved hearing it. He cherished these words each week, not knowing if it would be the last time he ever heard them.

David smiled. "I know, Dad. I love you too."

Later that night, David couldn't sleep. His body was tired, but his mind was racing. After about an hour of tossing and turning, Hailey woke up. "Are you still awake? What's wrong?" she asked.

"I was just thinking about Dad," David said quietly. "For some reason I have the most uneasy feeling. I can't stop wondering how many more conversations we're going to have."

Hailey put her head on his chest and wrapped her arm around him. "I know, baby. I think about that every Sunday as you two are on the phone."

David gripped Hailey tightly around her shoulder. "I guess it has just hit me all of a sudden that Noah probably won't ever get to know his own grandfather. My dad is the best man I know, but Noah won't even meet him. It's just really hard for me to accept that."

Hailey looked up at David and said with a smile, "Your dad is the second best man I know." She leaned up and gave him a kiss. Then she put her head back on his chest and went to sleep.

At 3:00 a.m. David's cell phone rang. He picked it up quickly. When he saw the name on the phone, his heart sank.

"Mom, what's wrong?" David asked with worry in his voice.

"It's your dad," his mom cried out. "He's gone."

CHAPTER 2

HIS FINAL GIFT

DAVID LOOKED DOWN at his watch. It was 6:55 p.m. "Wow," he thought, "have I really been standing here for almost three hours?" Even though he was physically and emotionally drained from all that he and his family had gone through over the last few days, David was surprisingly happy. He couldn't believe how many people had shown up for his dad's funeral service. The receiving of friends had already been going on for three hours, and there was still a line of people out the door. David had an odd sense of pride swell up inside him. "My dad truly was special," he thought to himself.

This was the perfect ending to what had been a horrible nightmare for David the last few days. It was the closure he needed. One by one people came through the line to pay their respects to a great man. Some of them had the nicest things to say about his dad. David relished their words. With each compliment they gave or quick funny story they told, David grew more and more proud. At one point, Hailey later told him, "He looked like he was beaming up there."

Even though David grew up in this area of Atlanta and spent his entire childhood in this same church, he had been gone for many years. A few of the people he knew really well. Many of them he simply recognized, or vaguely remembered their names as they came through the line. But most of these people he had never met. But whether he knew them or not, he enjoyed their kind words.

David felt a light tap on his shoulder. Pastor Rick was standing there with a loving smile on his face. "Just a few more minutes, OK? We need to go ahead and start the service soon."

"Yes, sir. Thank you," David replied.

Pastor Rick had been at this church since David was a teenager. When David gave his life to Jesus at age thirteen, Pastor Rick baptized him. When he went on his first mission trip at age sixteen, Pastor Rick took him. When he and Hailey got married after college, Pastor Rick officiated the service. David loved and respected him immensely. And now, all of these years later, it was Pastor Rick who would perform his dad's funeral service.

"You know, son, your dad was the real deal. He was a godly man. This church is going to miss him," Pastor Rick said with one hand on David's shoulder.

"Thank you for all of your help the last couple of days," David replied as he leaned in and hugged his pastor.

"Why don't we let a few more people come through and I will go ask the rest to take a seat?" Pastor Rick said lovingly. David really appreciated how he took charge and made everything so much easier on the family. After they pulled back from their hug, Pastor Rick walked down the line and respectfully asked everyone to take and seat for the start of the service. David looked down the line. There were six people remaining.

"Hey, David, my name is Dana," said the next gentleman in line. David didn't recognize him. He was a tall man who sounded like he was from the northeast. In the south, this guy's accent definitely stood out.

"I have been Tom's barber for many years," Dana continued.

"Barber!" David thought quietly to himself. "I can't believe a barber would show up to a funeral."

The barber continued, "Tom was a good guy. He sat in my chair every month for more years than I can remember. After a while, you get to know a person, you know?" Tears started to swell up in his eyes. "When I moved down here to Atlanta, I didn't know many people. Your dad was good to me. He treated me like family. He invited me to church and really made a big impact on my life, you know?"

Dana stopped to wipe the tears from his eyes. "Anyways, Tom talked about you all of the time. It's weird because we never met, but I feel like I know you. He always bragged about what you were doing."

"Dana, I can't thank you enough for coming out tonight," David replied. "It means a lot to me, what you said."

Dana wiped his tears one last time and cleared his throat. "I wanted to pay my respect. The world needs more guys like Tom." Dana quietly turned and walked away.

David turned back and instantly recognized the next man in line, but couldn't recall his name.

"Hey, David, John Patterson," he said as he shook his hand.

David quickly remembered. "John, yes! Good to see you again, sir."

"David, I know I have to be brief with the service about to start. But your dad and I went on several mission trips together," John said.

David interrupted, "Oh, did you go on all of those trips to Nicaragua?"

"Sure did!" John said with a big smile. "Tom was one of the hardest-working guys I have ever seen. I can't tell you how hard we worked down there in extreme heat. But of course, you know Tom, he never complained. Anyway, people are waiting so I'll go. I am very sorry for your loss."

"Thank you for coming, John," David said with a smile as they shook hands.

The next guy in line looked to be in his early twenties. David had never seen him before. He was clearly the youngest guy in the room. He looked nervous and out of place. David took charge.

"Hey, buddy, my name is David. I don't think we've met," David started as he took the young man by the hand.

"I'm Jacob," the young man said quietly.

After a moment of awkward silence, David said, "Well, thank you for coming, Jacob. How did you know my dad?"

Jacob looked like he wanted to say something. He didn't make much eye contact with David, and he couldn't stand still. Finally he looked up and said with a quiet voice, "Tom is my mentor. Or he was my mentor, I guess. Sorry."

David looked shocked. He talked to his dad every week on the phone, but he had no idea that he was mentoring young men.

"Really?" David asked with curiosity. "What do you mean?"

Jacob looked back down as he continued, "A few years ago, I got into drugs real bad. I dropped out of high school, and my life was all messed up. But a friend of mine told me that this church had a recovery program, so I checked it out. After I went through some classes, they hooked me up with a mentor to help me out. That's when I met Tom. We have been meeting together once a month for almost a year. I can honestly say he changed my life." Jacob looked at David in the eyes for the first time and added, "Without your dad I don't know where I would be right now."

David didn't know what to say. He was completely caught off guard. Overcome with emotion and an instant connection to this young man, David simply opened his arms and gave Jacob a hug. Jacob flinched at first, but then put one arm around David. It was the shortest hug ever, but it meant so much to David.

"Anyway, I'm kind of nervous," Jacob said as he looked back down. "I've never been to a funeral before. I'm sorry about Tom. See you around." With that, Jacob turned and left. He didn't stay for the service. He just waked right out and never looked back.

As David was watching Jacob leave, he heard a voice say, "Hello, David, I'm Jim Caldwell." David turned and saw a very well-dressed man in his fifties. His name sounded very familiar, but he didn't recognize his face.

"Hi, Jim," David said politely. "Thank you for coming tonight."

"I wouldn't miss it, David," Jim said enthusiastically. "Tom has been a client of mine for years."

David suddenly remembered the name. "Jim Caldwell is dad's financial advisor," David said to himself.

Jim never let go of David's hand as he continued, "Your dad was a very smart man. I've enjoyed working with him, and of course your mother. My job can be very stressful at times, but Tom was always fun and lighthearted."

"My dad has been telling me for years that I need to call you." David said.

"Now is not the time for that," Jim quickly replied. "I am always happy to help you, but I just wanted to say that I am very sorry for your family's loss."

"Thank you so much, Jim," David said with appreciation.

The next to last guy in line was a short African American man about David's age. He was in incredible shape. Even though he was dressed in a shirt and tie, David could still see his muscles.

"I'm Andre," the man said with a big smile on his face. He had a very outgoing personality and a glow about him.

"Andre?" David replied with curiosity. "You train my dad, right?"

"Yes, sir," said Andre. "Tom and I have been working out together for about two years.

"Well, you obviously know what you are doing," David joked as the grabbed Andre's muscular arm.

Andre laughed. "Yeah, well, I have to work hard to keep up with people like your dad. Tom pushed us all at the gym. Even during these last few months with his cancer, he still worked as hard as anyone."

"Yeah, health has always been very important to him," David said as he lowered his tone back to normal. "I never thought a health-related issue would kill him."

"It's a shame," Andre said. He still had a smile on his face, but somehow it was comforting.

Andre continued, "I was just telling your mom your dad led me to Christ a few weeks ago. I don't know if he told you or not."

"What? No, he didn't," David smiled. "That's incredible. Congratulations."

"Thank you," said Andre, still smiling. "Tom stayed on me for a while. But a few weeks ago, I was finally ready to listen. I gave my life to Jesus right there in my gym. It was amazing!"

"Andre, thank you so much for sharing that. It truly just made my day."

Andre leaned in and gave David a quick hug. Then he took a seat on the second row.

As David turned back, he saw the final person in line. He was giving his mom a long hug. It was Mike Brady. Mike and Tom were coworkers and best friends. David had known him since he was a kid. They had dinners together, vacationed together; Mike was practically family.

When David made eye contact with Mike, his emotions changed quickly. Mike's eyes were red and watery. He and David didn't even talk; they didn't need to. Mike just walked over and grabbed him. He was a large man, so David sank into his chest. David was suddenly overcome with emotions, and he began to weep. He hadn't cried this hard since his mom had called to deliver the bad news four days earlier. The sanctuary was silent. The only sound was of two grown men sobbing.

After a few minutes, Mike and David began to talk. They were oblivious to the fact that the funeral service was waiting on them to start, or that everyone was quietly watching them. They were in their own world. After several minutes of talking, Mike hugged David one last time and then sat down on the front row next to Ann, who had already taken her seat.

David slowly walked over and sat down next to Hailey. As the music began to play, she leaned over and whispered in his ear. "What did you and Mike talk about for so long?" she asked.

David turned and looked at Hailey. With a tear running down his cheek, he simply said one word, "Integrity."

After the funeral service, David and Hailey drove back to his parents' house. Ann asked them to stay because she wasn't ready to be alone. It had been a very long and emotionally exhausting day. They family was glad to finally be alone and quiet. Hailey gave David a kiss and said, "It's ten thirty, baby. I'm going to bed. My feet can't handle all of this extra weight."

"Good night, honey," David replied. "I'll be there soon."

Hailey gave Ann a hug and headed upstairs. It was quiet.

"He's really gone, isn't he, David?" Ann asked.

"Yes, ma'am," was all he replied.

"Mom," he added. "Are you going to be OK? I mean I know dad left you a large life insurance policy, but I'm not talking about money. I just mean, are you going to be fine?" David didn't exactly know how to say it.

"Honey, I am shell-shocked right now. There is no denying that," she answered. "But in time, I will be fine. Tom is with Jesus now. And as much as I will miss him, I know he is happy. I know he isn't sick anymore. Please don't you worry about me. You have a wife and baby to worry about now."

"Dad isn't the only strong one in the family," David said with a wink.

After a few seconds, Ann broke the silence. "Oh, I almost forgot. I have something for you." Ann walked out of the room and returned a couple of minutes later. She was carrying a box. On the side of the box was written the word: David.

"What is it?" David asked with curiosity.

"It's a gift," Ann quickly replied. "Your dad wanted you to have this."

"From Dad?" David said confused. Then suddenly he remembered his last conversation with his dad on Sunday night. "I just remembered, Dad said something on Sunday about having something for me. Is this it?"

"Yes." She nodded. "Dad has been working on this for a long time. He was so excited about it. Actually I don't think I have ever seen him more excited about anything in my life. He was going to give it to you when we came to Louisville for Noah's birth. He knew that he probably didn't have much more time, so he wanted to give it to you while he could."

David took the box from his mom. He didn't open it. He just held it in silence. It was light. He was so curious as to what was inside.

Ann continued as she started to cry, "He wanted more than anything to see your face when you open it. He wanted to go through the box with you. But I'm just glad that he finished it."

"Finished what?" he asked.

"You'll see, honey," she said with a sneaky grin. "I don't want to ruin it for you."

David walked over to the sofa and sat down with the box in his lap. For some reason he was nervous to open it. He just looked at it.

"Honey, why don't I leave you alone?" Ann said as she broke the silence. "I'm tired. I think I'll go on to bed."

David quickly set the box down on the table and rushed over to his mom. He gave her a long hug. "Good night, Mom. I love you." He kissed her on the forehead.

"I love you, too, David," she said with a smile on her face. "Enjoy your gift. I hope Dad can see this."

Ann went to bed, and David returned to his seat. He picked up the box and put it in his lap. He couldn't remember the last time he was this excited to open a gift. After a few seconds, he slowly opened the lid, set it on the floor, and looked inside.

David reached inside and pulled out a picture. He immediately recognized it. It was one of his favorite pictures of all time. It was a photo of him and his dad at the baseball field. David still remembered that day vividly. It was the first time his dad took him to an Atlanta Braves baseball game. In the picture David and his dad were standing right in front of the first base dugout. The field was in the background, and his favorite player, Chipper Jones, was standing right behind them on deck. They both have on Braves hats and shirts.

"I was six years old," David said quietly to himself. David loved this picture. Even though he and his dad went to numerous Atlanta Braves games over the years, including several playoff games and even one World Series game, that was still his favorite memory from that ballpark.

David had had this same picture hanging in his bedroom for many years. He couldn't remember exactly when he had taken it down, or why. But he remembers putting it in a junk drawer in his room one day when he was in high school.

"How did dad even get this picture?" he thought to himself.

David set the picture down on the coffee table and reached back in the box. He pulled out a stack of three-by-five index cards held together by a large clip. David instantly knew what they were.

Even though he was the only one in the room, David said aloud, "I can't believe he kept of these." It was a stack of Success Mottos. When David was a young boy, his dad started putting Success Mottos on his bathroom mirror. He would write them on white three-by-five index cards. At the top of the card, it said, "Success Motto." Then he would write a positive message or proverbial saying. He put up a new motto on David's mirror each week. He constantly told David to read the mottos when he brushed his teeth each morning and night. His dad would say things like, "Fill your mind with positive messages," and, "Successful people think thoughts of success."

David smiled as he took the clip off and started reading the cards. Some of them he actually remembered.

"Accepting responsibility for your actions is one of the hardest of all self-disciplines."
"You can't hire someone else to do your push-ups for you. You must do them yourself."
"Never settle for less than God's best for your life. God made you awesome!"
"It's better to try hard and fail than to not even try at all. Failure is OK; laziness is not."
"There is nothing more powerful than the mind. Whatever you think about, that's what you will become."

There were easily over two hundred cards in all. After reading them all, David put the clip back on the cards and set them on the table on top of the picture. When he looked back in the box, he said out loud, "Is that my old Bible?" He pulled out an old, worn-out Bible. He smiled as memories started flooding his mind.

David's parents had given him this Bible when he was thirteen on the day he was baptized. This Bible was very special to David. Throughout middle school and high school, this was the only Bible he used. He took it to church every Sunday morning. He took it to youth group each Wednesday night. He took it to summer camps, weekend retreats, and mission trips. It was filled with notes, underlined sentences, and high-lighted words. David suddenly recalled the first time he led one of his best friends to Christ using the Roman Road scriptures.

David was so lost in fun memories that he almost didn't notice the engraved words at the bottom of his old Bible. It said: Noah Williams.

He sat stunned with his mouth open, staring at the name. David couldn't believe it. His dad had actually taken his old Bible and engraved Noah's name on it. "What a great legacy!" David thought to himself. "What a great gift to one day give my son—my old Bible." He opened up the front cover of the Bible and saw a note. It read: *Noah, I pray that you will learn to love this book as your father did. May it be a lamp for your feet and a light for your path.*

The fun memories he had been thinking about while looking at the baseball picture and the mottos were suddenly changed to sadness. The fact that his son would never meet his dad was more than he could han-dle. David gripped the Bible tightly and prayed silently.

After a few minutes, he set the Bible down on top of the index cards and picture and looked back into the box. There were two more items. The first was a stack of three leather books bound together with a large rubber band. He took off the rubber band and saw that all three books looked exactly the same. He opened the first book and quickly realized that these were not just books; they were handwritten journals.

The inside cover of the first book said, "David's Journey." He turned to the first page and noticed that the date of the first entry was the day he was born. It read:

Dear David,

As I'm writing this I'm sitting in the hospital. Your mom is taking a much-needed nap after a long, hard day of pushing. You are asleep in the baby bed next to me. I can't stop looking at you. I can't believe that you are my son. You are so beautiful. The delivery went smoothly, and you and Mom are both healthy. Your mom yelled at me a couple of times during the painful delivery, but let's keep that between us. Anyway, I just wanted to start your life journal by saying that I love you.

At first David had not realized what these three books were, but now he understood. These were journals of his entire life. David was filled with a mixture of complete shock and excitement. He couldn't wait to read the journals. Out of curiosity David grabbed the third journal and turn to the very back page. The last journal entry was about his graduation from seminary. David couldn't believe it. His dad had literally journaled the first twenty-five years of his life.

It was too late to start reading them now, so he put the rubber band back around the journals and set them down on the coffee table next to the other gifts. He yawned. It was now after midnight, and he was exhausted. He reached in and pulled out the last item in the box. It was a solid black spiral-bound notebook. "What is this?" David wondered. He couldn't imagine anything better than the journals.

He opened up the cover and saw something completely unexpected. Written in his dad's messy handwriting, which David knew so well, it said, "David, this is my final gift to you."

David was stunned and confused. He thought that the entire box was the gift. "But could this notebook be what dad was referring to Sunday night?" he thought to himself. He was very eager to find out, so he turned the page and began to read.

David didn't know it yet, but his life was about to change.

CHAPTER 3

DEAR DAVID

David, I don't exactly know how to begin this letter. I know what I want to say, but I hope that I am able to communicate it well. I am dying. That is the first time I have ever written or spoken those words. It pains me to even write them, but I can't run from the truth. You know me, son. I'm an eternal optimist. I believe strongly in the power of the human mind. Whatever a person thinks about, he or she usually brings about.

It has been very hard for me to accept the fact that this cancer is going to take my life. I have tried my best to stay positive and joyful for your mom's sake. You know how she hangs on my every word. I just don't want her to worry. And I have complete faith that if the Lord wants to, He can remove this tumor and heal my body.

But I have finally decided to accept some very difficult realities:

1. *I have only a few more weeks or months to spend with my sweet bride.*
2. *I will not get to watch my grandson grow up.*
3. *I will not get to watch you become a father.*

And this is the purpose of this notebook. David, I know how nervous you are about becoming a father. I want more than anything to be there for you and help you along the way. But since God has other plans for me, I wanted to give you some things now while I still can. I can't think of anything more valuable that I can leave you with than this.

I am not a great writer, and there are certainly much better fathers out there than me. But I want to leave you with the most important lessons that I have learned about being a father. This is not a complete list, but it's my list. And I want you to have it. Do not feel obligated to use and apply every single lesson. But I believe that many of them, if not all of them, will greatly add value to your life.

You are going to be a great father, David. If I can't be with you physically, then maybe I can live through the words on these pages. I have told you hundreds of times since you were a young boy that my greatest calling in life is to raise you to become a godly young man. With the Lord's help, your mom and I have done that. And now it's your turn.

This is my final gift to you. I love you, and I have always been so proud to be your father. Always remember three things son:

Number one: You are special!

Number two: God loves you!

Number three: Daddy loves you!

A tear fell and landed on the page. David quickly dried it off with his sleeve before it ruined the paper. He was sobbing uncontrollably. He couldn't believe what he was holding in his hands. These were the final words of his father, mentor, and hero. David was surprised by how many pages there were in the notebook. He turned to the back and saw that the final lesson was #25.

"Twenty-five lessons from the best dad in the world," David thought to himself. "This is exactly what I need."

CHAPTER 4

LESSON 1: FATHERS ARE SO IMPORTANT

DAVID, I CAN'T think of a better lesson to start with than this one. Even though none of the twenty-five lessons that I want to share with you are in any certain order of value, I want to start with this one on purpose. If you gain nothing else from my gift to you, please at least take this lesson with you forever. Your role as a father is the greatest calling on your life.

The role of the father has changed so much over the decades. Throughout time, the father has always been the nucleus of the family. As the father went, so went his wife and children. But so much has changed. I read recently in *The New York Times* that one-third of all children in our great country are being raised without a father at home. This breaks my heart, son.

Children don't just need a dad; they need a father. And there is a big difference. Anyone can be a dad. I know that you have seen it happen many times in student ministry where two high school kids will unwisely fool around and unexpectedly get pregnant. This high school kid is now technically a dad. But he is not necessarily a father. Becoming a dad is easy, but being a father is difficult and it requires much work.

Our culture has nearly destroyed the role of the father. In most TV shows and movies, dads have been reduced and their reputations tarnished. Even in family sitcoms, kids' shows, and cartoons, fathers are no longer fathers. They are just dads, and it's sad. In these shows fathers are usually portrayed as either:

- completely absent from their kids' lives,
- the goofy, clueless guy who never knows what's going on, or
- a pushover who is the brunt of everyone's jokes.

I fear that is this trend will continue. The role of the father will continue to be minimized. But don't listen to this lie, David. You can't control the culture and you can't change others, but you can determine what your role will be as a father. You can control your family situation. *You* are so important. Great fathers are so needed in our society to be good examples to others. It is God who instituted marriage and established the family. It is God who created man first and gave him the responsibility as the head of his family. And it is God who created the important role of fathers and gave them this command in Ephesians 6:4: "Fathers…bring your children up in the training and instruction of the Lord."

David, there will be times when you feel inadequate as a father. There will be days when you are tired and you don't want to lead. There will be seasons of life where you will question if you are even making a difference. This is normal. I think all fathers feel this way at some point. When these moments happen, I encourage you to look to Scripture. Remember your role as a father. Remember the responsibility that God has given you to raise your precious son. Remember that you are the greatest influence in his life. There will be others along the way to help him grow as a person. He will have relatives, teachers, ministers, coaches, friends, and mentors, but none nearly as important and needed as you.

You alone are his father.

CHAPTER 5

LESSON 2: A BIBLICAL FOUNDATION

DAVID, LET ME tell you something that you already know. Your greatest gift to Noah, and any other children that God may give you in the future, is not a nice home, or a shiny new car on his sixteenth birthday, or even a full ride to college. The single most important thing that you can ever do for him is to give him a solid Biblical foundation. This of course flies in the face of our culture.

In our relativistic culture, people will often say things like...

"You believe what you want, and I'll believe what I want."

"Your way is right for you, and my way is right for me."

"All roads lead to heaven."

"Religion is too close-minded."

"The Bible is old school."

"You shouldn't indoctrinate your kids with a certain belief system."

As sad as this is, what else should we expect from an unbelieving culture? Of course they are going to live this way and believe these things. But what is truly sad, and I know that you have heard it often as a youth minister, is how many believers in the church will respond. Some Christian parents will say things like...

"I don't want to force my beliefs on my children."

"I want my children to make their own decisions about religion."

"I'm afraid if I make them to go church, then I will push them away."

"I want them to be free to choose their own way."

I don't mean to sound too harsh or critical. When Christian parents say things like this, they probably mean well. They certainly love their kids, but I think they are misguided. Years ago your mother and

I used to have these discussions often with many of our friends from church. Your mother would always give me little love tap under the table to remind me not to get all worked up. She is good like that. And I needed it because this is a passionate topic for me. I mean as Christian parents, what could possibly be more important than raising our children according to God's Word?

In response to some of our friends, I would simply ask them questions.

If you child was very sick and needed medicine, would you make her take it or let her decide?

If your son hated middle school and didn't want to go each day, would you force him to go anyway?

If your teenager asked you to go to a party where you knew there would be drugs and alcohol, would you let him go?

Do you truly believe that the Bible is God's Word?

Think about it, David. We, as parents, will do what we believe is best for our children even if they don't agree or understand. Whether they like it or not, we make them take their medicine and eat their vegetables because *we know* it's good for them. Whether they like it or not, we make them go to school each day because *we know* they need education and social skills. Whether they like it or not, we prevent them from going places where they could be harmed, or from hanging out with bad kids because *we know* that it's for their own good. So here's the kicker, David, for Christian parents who believe in the Bible: if *we know* that the Bible is relevant and life-changing, and if *we know* that a relationship with Jesus is the only way to heaven, then why wouldn't we want our children to *know* the same truth?

David, as godly man and minister, I know that this may sound obvious to you. Of course you want to give Noah a Biblical foundation. But all parents will one day come to a crossroad in life where they will have a defining moment. They must choose if they are going to raise their children according to God's word, or according to culture. My sincere prayer for you and Hailey is that you will respond to this defining moment the same way Joshua did. *"Now fear the Lord and serve Him with all faithfulness…But if serving the Lord seems undesirable to you, then choose for yourselves this day whom you will serve…But as for me and my household, we will serve the Lord." Joshua 24:14–15*

My favorite part of this passage is how Joshua says, *"…me and my household."* He was speaking on behalf of his family. I love this guy. He was a leader who did what was best for his family. He instilled in them truth and faith. Be that same leader, David. Be that same type of father. Regardless of what society teaches, or culture believes, or even how other weaker Christian parents raise their kids, you give Noah a strong Biblical foundation. You, and you alone, are responsible for the wife that you married and the children that God blesses you with.

Here are some of my favorite Bible verses on building a solid Biblical foundation for your family:

*Deuteronomy 6:6–9
"These commandments that I give you today are to be upon your hearts. Impress them on your children. Talk about them when you sit at home and when you walk along the road, when you lie down and when you get up. Tie them as symbols on your hands and bind them on your foreheads. Write them on the doorframes of your houses and on your gates."
Create a household where God is honored and his Word is discussed.

*Psalm 119:105
"Your word is a lamp to my feet and a light for my path."
We live in a dark and evil world. Give your son the light by teaching him the truth in Scripture.

*Proverbs 22:6
"Train a child in the way he should go, and when he is old, he will not turn from it."

All children will sin and make bad decisions. Some may even rebel for a while. But if your child knows Jesus, then God will bring him back.

*Hebrews 10:25

"Let us not give up meeting together, as some are in the habit of doing, but let us encourage one another."

Make church, small groups, and other Christian gatherings a priority. When life gets busy, don't sacrifice these opportunities to be around like-minded believers.

CHAPTER 6

LESSON 3: I LOVE YOUR MOTHER

DAVID, OF ALL of the lessons that I want to teach you about being a great father, this one is both the easiest and the most difficult at the same time. I say easy, of course, because there is nothing better than being in love. I know that Hailey is your best friend and greatest joy. But this lesson can be very difficult, too, son. Marriage is beautiful, but it can also be very hard at times. The person you love the most in this world can hurt your heart and disappoint you more than any other.

So what does this have to do with being a father? Everything. You know the nasty statistics better than me. You live it every day with students in your ministry. Divorce is devastating. Depending on which statistic you read, somewhere between 40 percent and 50 percent of first marriages will end in divorce. What we, as men, need to truly understand are the life-changing effects that a failed marriage can have on children. Consider these horrible but true statistics from Focus of the Family's website as they studied the differences between children from divorced homes compared to children from married homes.

- Children from divorced homes suffer academically. Their grades are typically lower and they experience more behavior problems at school.
- Children from divorced homes are more likely to commit a crime as a juvenile.
- Children from divorced homes are more likely to live in poverty.
- Teenagers from divorced homes are more likely to engage in drugs, alcohol, and sexual activity.

- Children from divorced homes experience more psychological distress and are in greater need of emotional counseling.
- Children from divorced homes experience more frequent illness and develop more health problems.

These statistics break my heart, son. They prove that a failed marriage can literally devastate a child for many years. But they also give us an important reminder of how a strong marriage can positively affect children for the rest of their lives. You can't change these statistics, but you can control our own destiny. You can determine that you and Hailey will have a solid marriage and that Noah will be blessed because of it.

Before you can become a great father, you must first learn to be a great husband. Remember, there is only one person on this planet that you committed to spend the rest of your life with, and that is your wife. *God* chose to give you a son, but *you* chose your wife. I want to share one of my favorite verses in the Bible. Ephesians 5:25 says, "Husbands, love your wives, just as Christ loved the church and gave himself up for her." It's easy for a husband to love his wife physically. In fact, physical touch is the highest love language for most men. But the comparison in this verse is about how Jesus loves his followers. This is a kind of love that is sacrificial, forgiving, unconditional, and most of all, eternal. This is how husbands should love their wives. This is how you should love Hailey. And this is how Noah should see his dad loving his mom.

I want to give you some marriage advice, David, on how to show your kids that you love their mother. I wish someone would have shared this with me when I was in my twenties and thirties.

1. BE AFFECTIONATE IN PUBLIC.

When children are little, they usually say it's "yucky" to see Mom and Dad kissing. When they are teenagers, they say it's "embarrassing." But I believe that deep down in their hearts, all kids love to see that their parents love each other. I'm not talking about tasteless public displays of affection that make every passerby uncomfortable. I simply mean that it is healthy for your kids to see you being loving and affectionate with your wife.

Kiss her when you walk in the door from work. Hold her hand as you sit in the car. Put your arm around her in church. Cuddle up next to her on the couch. Hug her tightly when she shares good news. Massage her shoulders when she's had a bad day. Play with her hair as you watch a family movie together at home. And do all of these things in front of your kids. Kids need to see that Dad loves Mom, especially boys. Boys need a positive example of what it should look like for a man to show affection to a woman in a modest and respectful manner.

2. ARGUE IN PRIVATE.

You've heard it said that there are only two certainties in life: death and taxes. Well, I think there is a third. You will, at times, argue with your spouse. It's a part of marriage, but it needs to be done wisely and tactfully. David, I encourage you to the best of your ability to keep your arguments with Hailey as private as possible.

It's OK that you disagree in front of the kids, or if you have an occasional spiff. See to it that when this happens, you treat it as a learning experience. Set a good example by apologizing to Hailey (in front of Noah) if you were out of line. Or you may even need to apologize to Noah for treating his mother disrespectfully. Either way, you can easily turn a negative experience into a positive one.

Don't be "that couple," son. Don't be that couple who screams and yells at each other in front of their kids. Don't be that couple who uses vulgar or inappropriate language in order to hurt their spouse. Don't be that couple who is focused more on winning the argument than making it right. Don't be the couple who slams doors or walks away angry.

Remember, your kids watch everything you do and say. The way you treat your wife during an argument or disagreement will have a lasting effect on how your son will treat his future wife. So be tactful and exercise good judgment. When you argue, and you will, do it in private.

3. PRAY FOR HER IN FRONT OF YOUR KIDS.

There is perhaps no greater way to show your love for someone than by praying for them. I know that you pray for Hailey often. But as Noah gets older, I encourage you to pray for her with him. Your kids need to hear you pray, period. You are the spiritual leader in your home. Pray for her out loud so that your kids can hear your heart. Pray for your marriage. Pray for her at work. Pray for her when she has bad days. Pray for her when she has something important coming up. Pray for her when she is sick. But above all, just thank God for who she is.

4. COMPLIMENT HER.

1 Thessalonians 5:11 says, *"Encourage one another and build each other up."* If this is true in the Church, then it should also be true in the home. Our words are so important. They can either give life, or destroy life. Make a conscious effort to compliment your wife in front of your kids. Not only is this good for your marriage, but it is very beneficial for your kids as well. They need to hear things like:

> *You look beautiful today.*
> *That dress looks great on you.*
> *Thank you for making the house look so good.*
> *Dinner is incredible.*
> *I appreciate your hard work ethic.*
> *You are having the best attitude today.*
> *You are such an amazing mother.*

When kids hear these words from their father to their mother, it gives them comfort. Nearly half of their friends come from a broken home, and even more have parents who criticize each other publically. When you encourage and compliment your wife, you are indirectly telling your kids that you love their mother. And all kids desperately need to know that.

5. BE ON THE SAME TEAM.

Do you remember your wedding day? What about your wedding vows? I don't have much memory of my own, but I can recall yours vividly. I remember telling your mother that day that you two are perfect for each other. It's as if you were literally created for each other. Genesis 2:25 says, *"For this reason a man will leave his father and mother and be united to his wife, and they will become one flesh."*

I love this verse because it teaches us not only that God created marriage to be permanent, but also that marriage is about unity. To put it in my own basic terms, you and your wife are on the same team. You are one. You need to live out this truth with your kids. I have seen too many kids, especially teenagers, who will actually divide their parents. They will pick sides, play favorites, and in doing so can accidentally turn one against the other.

Teach your kids that you and your wife are on the same team. Make important decisions together. Support each other's choices in front of the kids. Say things like: *"Mom and I will discuss it and let you know. If your mom said no, then I say no. We need to pray about that first. I support her decision. Don't come to me just because you don't like her answer."* Kids won't like every decision that you and Hailey make, but at least they will know that you are on the same team, no matter what.

6. SHARE LOVE STORIES.

Telling stories is one of the most powerful and effective ways to teach. Jesus often taught his disciples and the crowds using parables and stories. By telling your son stories about you and Hailey, you can indirectly teach him so many great lessons about being a gentlemen and how to treat a lady. Kids need to know their family heritage. They need a legacy to carry on.

Whether they admit it or not, they want to hear your stories. Tell them how you met and started dating. Share some of your funny, embarrassing, or even romantic moments. Explain what it means to pursue a woman the right way. Teach them how to court a woman. By telling stories, not only can you pass on your heritage and legacy, but more importantly, you can indirectly teach your son how to treat a lady.

7. INVOLVE THE KIDS IN FUN SURPRISES FOR HER.

I don't know many things, son, but one thing that I know for certain is that it's the little things in life that mean the most. This cancer has caused me to do a lot of thinking and reflecting. When I think back to some of my most favorite memories, many of them were just fun little surprises that you, your mom, and I did together. If you really want to make a lasting impression on Noah, then involve him in your fun, little surprises for Hailey.

If you're going to buy her flowers, then take him with you to pick them out. If you're going to write her a sweet letter or card, then get him to sign it. If you're going to plan a fun date, then ask him for ideas. If you're shopping for a special gift for her, then get him to help you search online. The point, David, is that if you involve your kids in the silly little, fun things, then you can show them how you put time, thought, and creativity into your wife. Your kids will see and know that their dad really cares about their mom. And since they will be a part of it, they will carry those memories into their own marriages one day.

8. DATE HER REGULARLY.

There is nothing better than being a father, David, as you will soon learn. In fact, all of these lessons that I'm writing for you are about being the best father that you can be for Noah and any other children that God may bless you with. But please, son, do not neglect your wife. Your first love and first commitment is to your spouse.

I have seen far too many couples that are good parents, but somewhere along the way, they forgot how to love each other. Many of my friends have gotten divorced after their kids grew up and moved out and they suddenly realized that they hardly knew each other. The best way I know how to make sure that this never happens to you and Hailey is to make dating a priority in your marriage. Date her regularly. Come up with your own schedule, but make sure it's consistent and often. It does not matter whether it's a weekly date night, every other week, or even once a month, but please make it at least once a month.

Your kids need to know that you love each other, that you enjoy being together, and that you need alone time. And tell them why you're doing it. Say things like, "I'm taking my hot wife out on a date tonight." Or, "Your mother and I really want to spend some alone time together, so we're going on a weekend trip." Find out what works best for you and stick to it. The purpose is to show your son that no one is more important to you than your wife. And when you date her regularly, he will know that you really mean it.

CHAPTER 7

LESSON 4: THE JOURNAL

DAVID, I AM about to say three words that most men don't want to hear: *keep a journal.* Journaling seems to come more natural for women than it does for men. Maybe we are too masculine. Maybe we think that writing out our thoughts and feelings is weird. Maybe the idea of journaling reminds us of a little girl writing in her diary. Whatever the reasons, they are silly and immature.

Journaling is a powerful way to capture the past so that you will never forget it. Take it from me, son, the older you get, the less you remember. It's crazy. Sometimes your mother and I will laugh because we can't remember some of the most important events in our lives. I can vaguely recall my wedding day, but with very few details. Sometimes I will look at my college diploma on my wall at home and question if I actually went to college. I can hardly remember any of it. It's sad, but true. We were married for more than five years before you were born, but the details of those years seem so vague.

Lesson #4 is to keep a Life Journal for Noah. Since you are reading this now, one of two things has already happened. Either I gave you the box myself, or I have gone to be with Jesus so your mother gave it to you. Either way, by now you probably know about the journals that I have for you. The reason I started journaling your life is because I didn't want to forget you. You are the greatest blessing that God has ever given your mom and me. We may have forgotten many of the important memories in our own lives, but we didn't want to lose any of yours.

I want you to do the same thing for Noah, and any others kids you many have. Keep a journal of their lives. There are a lot of really great gifts that we can give our kids as they get older. We can buy them a car, or pay their college tuition, or even help them furnish their first apartment or house. But I can't think of a better gift than to hand your son a journal of his entire life. It's literally priceless. That's why I started your journal. I not only wanted you to have your childhood memories on paper, but I wanted to share with you what I was actually thinking, feeling, and experiencing in that moment. I wanted you to have my words. I wanted to be able to help you, teach you, guide you, and sometimes just make you laugh. More than anything, I wanted you know how proud of you I am and how much I love you.

I am no expert on journaling, and to my knowledge there isn't a rulebook on how to do it. But I encourage you to simply start. Buy a journal right now and just start writing. When Noah does something funny, write it down. When you guys enjoy a great memory, write it down. When he messes up and you want him to learn an important lesson, write it down. When you experience anything for the first time, write it down. When you are worried about him or are struggling about something, write it down. When he accomplishes something incredible, write it down. And try to keep things like pictures, ticket stubs, movie tickets, sweet little notes, drawings, etc. Paper clip them next to the journal entry.

When and how you give the journal to him is up to you. I have thought many times about it. I almost gave you your journals when you graduated from high school, but I decided that you were not mature enough yet. I almost gave them to you after you got married but decided that it wasn't the right time. I almost gave them to you the day you got ordained in ministry, but I just didn't feel a peace about it. Maybe I was wrong. Maybe I should have already given them to you. And I sure would like to see your face when you read them.

But you will know what's right for Noah. You will know when he is ready to receive it. My greatest advice about the journal is don't ever quit writing. Don't allow laziness to creep in. Don't let too much time pass in between each entry. Don't talk yourself out of it because it's too big of a project. Don't neglect to write something down simply because it's not important enough. Trust me, if it's about Noah, then it's important. By the way, I really hope that you enjoy reading your journals. I started writing on the day you were born and I have literally written throughout your entire life. I can't even describe how much joy it has given me. I hope you feel same way as you read it. I love you so much, son.

CHAPTER 8

LESSON 5: ABOVE ALL, TEACH SELF-DISCIPLINE

If there is anything that fathers need to instill in their children, it is self-discipline. I believe that with the passing of each generation this all-important characteristic is becoming less and less prevalent, especially in the lives of young men. My horrible disease has caused me to do a lot of thinking and reflecting. When I consider my parents' generation and even my generation, and then compare them to today's generation, the area of self-discipline seems to be almost lost in the lives of young adults and teenagers. I am so proud that you are a man who models self-discipline, David. From the time you could barely talk, your mother and I worked tirelessly to teach you the value of this great character trait.

Above all else, teach Noah to become self-disciplined. Self-discipline is many things. To some people it's a negative word, and to others it's considered old-fashioned. I even have some friends who believe that people are either born with this trait or not; you can't teach it. Now you know, I don't believe that son, and neither should you. Self-discipline is a learned behavior; therefore, you must teach it to your children. To me, it means the power to control your own feelings and actions. It's about creating new habits of thought and action in order to improve yourself and your life.

It is very important that you start teaching this to your children at a young age, and that you stay consistent throughout their childhood. Self-discipline is extremely difficult to teach, but you must, David. The reason it is so valuable is because a father can tell his son what to do until he is blue in the face, but until the son learns to do things for himself, then he is not improving; he's just obeying. The key word is "self." It's all about personal accountability. Your son needs to learn and understand this phrase: "I am who I am, I am where I am, and I have what I have because of my decisions, period."

The absolute best way to teach your kids self-discipline is to first model it yourself. If you want Noah to eventually start creating habits that will improve his mind and body, then you must do it yourself. Self-disciplines are more *caught* than *taught* when it comes to adolescents. It will not always be easy or fun, but you must become a model of self-discipline. Don't try to be perfect; just try to get better. Discipline yourself to eat healthy and exercise regularly. Discipline yourself to read often and watch television less. Discipline yourself to wake up early and spend time with God. Discipline yourself to save money and bless others. Remember, your son wants to be just like you. As you work to improve yourself, you are by default improving your son.

The second best way to teach your kids self-discipline is to discuss it often at home. This isn't a speech that you give to a high school graduate as he is about to leave for college. It must be discussed often throughout his childhood and teenage years. Teach them that self-discipline is the foundation of all personal achievement. If they love sports or certain athletes, then make sure they understand how and why those people have accomplished so much. They weren't just born with a talent. They didn't get lucky. Rather, they worked hard, sacrificed much, and did what others were not willing to do. They are self-disciplined.

The third best way that your mother and I found to teach self-discipline is by recognizing and rewarding it when it happens. Always keep your eyes and ears open for opportunities to encourage your children by rewarding their good decisions. This can be difficult because our natural tendency is to focus only on the outcomes. But as you teach what it means to be self-disciplined and why it's so important, you must celebrate it when you see it. Develop your own system that works for you, but here are a few examples:

If he does his chore without being told, don't worry about whether or not he did a good job; compliment him for taking initiative on his own.

If he works really hard on a school project all week and hardly plays video games so that he can get it right, don't just focus on his grade; reward him for his effort.

If he makes his bed all week without being told, take him to get ice cream on Friday night.

If he chooses to read a book instead of watching TV, tell him you're proud.

If he always hustles hard on his sports team, but doesn't have much success, recognize his effort and hustle.

If you catch him reading the Bible or praying on his own, take him to get a special treat.

The point is, the more self-discipline is modeled yourself, the more you will focus on it. The more you focus on it, the more you will teach and expect it. The more you teach it, the more it will be learned and applied. The more it is applied, the more it needs to be recognized and rewarded. The more it is rewarded, the more it will be demonstrated. And the more it is demonstrated by your kids, the better they will become. Trust me on this, if you are able to teach Noah the value of self-discipline, then he will be way ahead of his peers and competitors as a young adult.

CHAPTER 9

LESSON 6: THE POWER OF REPETITION

LET ME TELL you a little secret that has the potential to literally change your life: there is so much power in repetition. I don't know if anything is more powerful and transforming to the human brain and the physical body than repetition. Your mother and I first learned this lesson when you were a young boy and we used it to subconsciously teach you so many great truths. I strongly encourage you to do the same for your son.

Let's take a fun, quick trip down memory lane. No one understands and utilizes the power of repetition better than good ole World Wrestling Entertainment. I'm not a big fan of these guys, but you used to watch it every week growing up. They are the masters of taking a few little phrases and repeating them over and over and over and over, until twenty thousand people in a stadium and literally copy the phrase in unison. It's the craziest thing I've ever seen. Grown men and women will stand up and shout these common catchphrases at the top of their lungs as if their lives depend on it. Wrestlers can get the audience to do and say whatever they want by using the secret power of repetition. You probably haven't seen or heard these catchphrases in many years, but I bet you remember them. Let's see...

- Hulk Hogan: "Whatcha gonna do, brother, when Hulkamania...
  runs wild on you."
- Stone Cold Steve Austin: "And that's the bottom line...cause
  Stone Cold said so"
- Rick Flair: "To be the man, WOOO...
  you gotta beat the man."

- The Rock: "Can you smell...
     what the Rock is cooking."

I'm guessing that you remembered them all. Repetition is not only powerful, but it can last a lifetime in the subconscious. Use this tool to teach, train, and mold Noah into a godly young man. The key is to start early. I remember when you were a little baby. Before you could even talk I used to say the same thing to you every night. I would say, "Can I tell you three things? You are special. God loves you. And Daddy loves you." I repeated these words to you almost every day (and I still do)!

When you were about four years old, we started using the power of repetition with Bible verses. Do you remember? Every Sunday night we would practice your Bible verses. We added one new verse per week, and sometimes when life got hectic, we would only add about one per month. But we stayed consistent. When you were five years old you could recite more than twenty Bible verses from memory. As a teenager, you knew more than one hundred verses. My guess is that you remember most of them even to this very day. Why? Repetition.

You can do this with anything. While many families never talk about money with their kids, we were teaching you money lessons before you could ride a bike. We used repetition to drive these lessons into the very fiber of your being. Every day when you completed your chore, we would pay you money for the work. As we handed you the money, we would say, "Work hard, get paid." When you wanted to take your earned money and immediately go and spend it all on something, we would say, "Always save some." When you took a small portion to give to the church, we would say, "Always tithe." When you ran out of money but still wanted to buy a toy, we would say, "Debt is bad." It's sad, but you probably knew more about money in elementary school than many adults. As you grew older, we added new money lessons and repeated them over and over.

When you started playing sports, we used this same strategy, and it worked. Before every game I repeated the exact same words to you. I said, "David, I want you to do three things: Listen to your coach. Run hard. And have fun." And you always did them. You knew what was important to me. You learned what sports were all about, and what they are not about.

I will give you one more example. From the time you were a child, as I tucked you in bed, I would often ask you the same question. After we talked and prayed I would ask, "Is there anything that you want to talk about?" I repeated this same question hundreds of times.

Most of the time you said, "No." But every once in a while you would surprise me by saying, "Yes, sir." These were the nights when we had special father-son talks about Jesus, girls, school, friends, morals, etc. I cherish these moments. I don't know if you would have had the courage to discuss these issues with me or not, if I hadn't asked you that same question over and over again. But I do believe that it's because of the power of repetition.

It's not important that you follow these exact examples, David. I am just trying to illustrate how powerful this teaching tool can be for you. What is important is that you and Hailey find what works best for you. Think about whatever is really important to you, and then repeat it over and over. Noah may eventually roll his eyes, or say, "Yeah, Dad, I got it." But continue. You can teach him whatever you want. You can mold him into the kind of man that you want him to become. With the power of repetition you can take any lesson, truth, or value and insert it into his subconscious mind. But remember, negative traits and lessons are just as easily learned through repetition. So choose wisely what you repeat.

CHAPTER 10

LESSON 7: THE VALUE OF MANNERS

DAVID, PLEASE ALLOW me to stand on my soapbox for a few minutes as we discuss the value of manners. Few things annoy me more than seeing a young man with no manners. Likewise, few things make me smile more than being in the presence of a young man with good manners. Manners can tell you as much about a person as almost any other trait or characteristic. One of the many reasons that I am so proud of you, son, is because you have always used good manners. Your mother and I made sure of it when you were younger, but even to this day, you are polite and respectful.

I hope so badly that I will live long enough to see young Noah develop his own set of manners. But, I know that you will teach him well. And that's what it takes, David. Manners are seldom learned except by the consistent effort of parents. But just in case God does not grant me the time to see it for myself, I want to leave you with some extremely important truths about manners. I have never claimed to be a smart man or a great father, but I know for a fact that if you apply these lessons, then your children will be better for it. Here are a few things that I have learned about manners.

1. MANNERS SHOULD BE SPECIFIC.

It is not enough to teach kids to just be polite or respectful. Parents should be much more specific. Kids cannot learn and apply what they are not taught. And the more specific parents are, the easier it is for kids to learn. I encourage you to make a specific list of the manners that are important to you. It may not be a complete list, but make one anyway. You have to start somewhere. Having a list will help keep you on track and remind you of which manners you need to focus on. When you were young, we hung a short list of manners on the refrigerator so that you could see it. But you don't have to display your list, just have one. When something is out of sight, then it is usually out of mind. Having a specific list of manners causes your mind to focus on it subconsciously, which will result in more teachable moments when the time arises.

There are hundreds of good manners to learn, but as you make your list, keep these in mind.

-May I please
-Eat over your plate
-Yes, sir or No, ma'am
-Clean up after yourself
-Don't talk with your mouth full
-Don't brag about yourself
-Have a firm handshake
-Say excuse me
-Return things that you borrow

-Thank you
-Chew with your mouth closed
-Open doors for people
-Compliment the cook
-Don't interrupt people
-Look people in the eyes when you talk
-Stand with good posture
-Remember people's names
-Don't make fun of people

2. MANNERS ARE OFTEN NEGLECTED.

When parents don't do a good job instilling manners in their kids, it's not because they don't find manners to be valuable. It's simply because of neglect. Everyone is busy. In fact, your generation has more expectations, responsibilities, and options than my generation did. Parents are working harder and longer, and kids are involved with more activities than ever before. So, in our busy, hectic, and chaotic lives, one of the values that is often set aside is manners. Teaching manners is difficult because it takes a purposeful and consistent effort. It doesn't just happen naturally. It can sometimes be easier for parents to allow reality TV, social media, and the Internet to raise their kids. When this happens, good manners are neither taught nor caught.

3. MANNERS MUST BE MODELED.

It isn't enough to just make a list of manners and teach them to your kids. You must also model them. Many parents operate with an attitude of "do as I say, not as I do." This is not helpful. It is confusing for kids when parents tell them to do something, but then they do the opposite. But when you teach and model good manners, your kids are likely to follow. Always look for teachable moments. When you open the door for a group of people, tell your young child to "come here and help me hold the door for these nice folks." When you walk away from a group of people, ask your son if he remembers their names, and why it's so important. When your wife makes a great meal and you give her a compliment, ask your son if there is anything he wants to say. Modeling good manners doesn't mean that you have to be perfect. So when you mess up, own it. That is also a teachable moment. Apologize if you interrupt your son when he is talking. Apologize if you burp and don't say excuse me. Kids can learn as much from failure as they do from success if it is handled well.

4. MANNERS NEED TO START EARLY.

It really is hard to teach an old dog new tricks. By the time people reach adulthood whatever manners they have, or don't have, will likely stay with them forever. It's important to start teaching manners early. Don't expect much response from toddlers, but start anyway. I have heard that it's easier to teach a young child a foreign language than an adult. The same is true for manners. By the time kids enter elementary school, they should have a solid foundation of good manners. They won't always remember to use them, but they are still aware of them. By middle school, kids should already have a reputation with teachers and coaches as being polite and respectful. Any by the time your son is in high school, manners should be second nature.

5. MANNERS ARE ATTRACTIVE.

One of the reasons you need to teach your son good manners to help him get ahead in life. This should be the goal of every parent. Children and teenagers with good manners are more attractive to adults. I don't mean physically better looking. I just mean that they are more likely to stand out in a positive way. When you instill good manners into your kids, everyone will take notice. Teachers will be more likely to offer extra help. Coaches will give you more attention and respect. The parents of your son's girlfriend will trust him more to take their daughter out. And down the road, employers will be quicker to hire and promote young men with good manners.

6. MANNERS SHOULD BE REWARDED.

Manners go against our human nature. We are sinful and selfish by nature, which is the exact opposite of good manners. Therefore teaching a child to have manners can be time consuming and frustrating. One tactic that works well is to reward good manners. When your child does something good, immediately acknowledge it and reward it. Rewards can be anything from a "good job," to a piece of candy or toy. One summer when you were about eight years old, we actually paid you for memorizing and using a certain list of manners. You wanted that money so badly. Your mother and I used to reward you every time another adult, teacher or parent would comment on how well-mannered you were. The bottom line is to catch kids doing good things and reward them for it. Over time their little minds will start to understand that good manners = good rewards. This truth will serve them well in adulthood.

7. MANNERS CREATE SELF-RESPECT.

Finally good manners make people feel good about themselves. It's the Golden Rule principle: Treat people the way you want to be treated. When kids have good manners and they start to become more aware of how they treat others, it naturally causes them to take pride in themselves. The better we treat others, the better we feel about ourselves. The more we show respect to people, the more self-respect we create within us. Manners are more than just about being nice or polite. At the core, it's about who you are as a person. When we teach our kids the value of manners, we are also helping them to love and respect themselves.

CHAPTER 11

LESSON 8: I'LL ALWAYS DO WHAT I SAY I'M GOING TO DO

DAVID, THIS LESSON is so very important. Please take it to heart and follow through with it. It should already be ingrained in your subconscious mind. You have not only lived through this lesson, but you heard me use this phrase thousands of times during your childhood. But knowing something and doing something are two different things. Everything changes when you become a father. Many of the lessons and values that you know to be true can easily go out the door. Compromise and convenience can often times become the rule, not the exception. Let me explain, son.

I have seen it a million times, and so have you. A father will say to his son, "If you don't stop arguing with me, I'm going to spank you." Then ten seconds later, "I said stop arguing." Moments later, "You better stop or you're going to get it." And what does the child continue to do? Argue. What does the dad do? Nothing. Who wins? The child. Or does he?

Or a mother will say to her young daughter, "If you don't stop crying, we are not going to go get ice cream." The daughter keeps crying. "I said you better stop. I'm serious, we'll go straight home." The daughter isn't happy, so she cries even louder. Then the mother starts counting. "I'm going to count to three, and if you don't stop, then we will not get ice cream. One…two…You better stop. I'm serious. One…two…three… what did I say?" The mother then looks at her friend beside her and starts laughing. "Kids!" she jokes. The other mother laughs. And you know the end of the story. The mother says good-bye to her friend, puts her daughter in the car, and they head off to get ice cream. Did the mother follow through with what she said? No. Who wins? The daughter. Or does she?

Or a father says to his teenage son, "You need to turn off the TV and go study for your test tomorrow."

The boy says, "I'll do it later. It's not hard."

The father says, "I'm serious, son. This test is a big deal. You have been slacking lately in school. You need to get your grades up."

"It's fine, Dad, I will in a minute," he replies.

The dad fires back, "I promise you, if you fail this test like you did the last one, you are not going to your friend's party tomorrow night." The next day the boy comes home with an F on his test. The dad says, "I told you, you are not going to the party tonight. I'm so frustrated with you."

"But, Dad, all of my friends will be there," he begs.

"No!" the father demands.

The boy knows how to play this game, so he goes to his mom and explains just how important this party is and how devastated he will be to miss it. The mom then goes to her husband and says, "Oh, come on, let him go. He really is sorry. He will be so sad if he misses the party."

"Fine," the father says in defeat. "But he needs to get his grades up." Did the father gain the respect of his son by letting him go to the party? No. Who wins? The son. Or does he?

I could go on and on with examples, but you get my point. So many parents fail their children by giving in, changing their minds, or compromising their word. So here is the lesson, David: Always do what you say you're going to do. The sad reality is that parents who go back on their word think that they are doing their child a favor. They think that they are making their child happy. But instead, they are teaching their child a dangerous lesson.

I know that you remember this, David, but when you were a young child your mother and I started using this important lesson in your life. Whenever you would do something that I told you not to, I would always say, "David, I love you, and I promise that I will always do what I say

I'm going to do." So if I said that a certain punishment would happen, then that's exactly what we did…every time. Anytime we said, "If you do _____, then we will do _____," we always came through on our word. But more than that, we always said those magical words first, "We love you and we promise that we will always do what we say we're going to do." When you were younger, I would usually drive the lesson home by asking a few questions. "David, did I say that if you didn't clean your room then you couldn't play video games?"

"Yes, sir," you would whimper.

"Did you clean your room?"

"No, sir," you would reply.

"Do I always do what I say I'm going to do?"

"Yes, sir," you would conclude.

"Then you can't play video games today."

Here is what I want to teach you, David. This is not about being a cruel dad or a drill sergeant. And it certainly doesn't mean that we can never change our minds or exercise grace with our kids. But what I want you to learn from this lesson is a complete paradigm shift in mentality. When you tell your son, "If you do ____, then I will do ____," you are not being a tough father. You don't want him to think, "My dad is so mean." Rather, you want him to think, "My dad doesn't lie." You see, when parents go back on their word, they are telling their kids indirectly that lying isn't that bad. When you were growing up, I wanted you to know that your dad was a man of character and integrity. My word meant something.

Again, it's important that your kids hear these specific words, or something similar. For them to understand the connection to honesty and integrity, then kids need to hear this phrase often. "I love you, and I promise that I will always do what I say I'm going to do." When you say these words, it also opens that door for a teachable moment, which parents should constantly be looking for. Over time, your son will soon realize that when his dad says something, he means it. Not because he is mean or stubborn, but because he is a man of honesty and character.

The coolest thing about your son learning this lesson over time is when he starts to use it against you. You used to do this and I loved it. You would say something like, "Hey, Dad, you said that we would go to the baseball field today."

"I know, buddy, but I am slammed with work today," I might say.

"But, Dad, you said that we would go, and you always do what you say you're going to do." You got me! What a perfect comeback. This worked every time you did it. I love it because I knew that you fully understand the purpose of the lesson. You believed that I am an honest man. And that, David, is why you must always do what you say you're going to do with your kids.

CHAPTER 12

LESSON 9: TRUST AND OPEN COMMUNICATION

EVERY PARENT DESIRES to have a close relationship with his or her child. Every mother wants her child to be able to talk to her about anything. Every father longs for his child to trust him completely. David, this lesson on trust and open communication is perhaps the easiest to do, and yet it is so rare to see it accomplished.

I thank God often that you and I have this rare gift of openness and honesty on all subjects. I know that you often come to me to discuss issues that you don't share with anyone else. I am so thankful for your trust and I cherish our private conversations. But it wasn't always this way. In fact, you were a tough nut to crack! When you were seven or eight years old, it was like pulling teeth to get anything of substance out of you. Most of our conversations were on the surface level only. I felt like you were holding back from telling me more. After much thought and prayer, I came up with a very simple solution. It may not seem like much, but I encourage you to apply this lesson with Noah.

Ask your child this question: *Is there anything you want to talk about?* I told you it was simple. When I started asking you this question, everything eventually changed in our relationship. You opened up and started talking more. It took quite a bit of time, but we started having some very special conversations. I'm sure by now you can probably remember me asking you this question when you were a teenager. I truly believe with all of my heart that we probably wouldn't have our weekly Sunday night phone call to this day if I hadn't started asking you this question as a young boy. As simple as it is to ask this question, there are a few more things that I want to say about it.

1. ONLY ASK THIS QUESTION ONE-ON-ONE AND IN PRIVATE.

This question is not for family discussions or dinner talk. The whole purpose is to create an environment of trust and openness. Don't ever ask it in front of his friends, or while the TV is on, or while his mind is occupied. Keep it purposeful. I recommend that you have a specific time and place that you ask him each time. Our time and place was in your bed right before you went to sleep. This worked best for us, but find a time and place that works best for you.

2. FROM TIME TO TIME, EXPLAIN WHY YOU'RE ASKING THIS QUESTION.

It's not enough to simply ask, "Is there anything you want to talk about?" You should explain why you're asking him. Of course you are interested in his day-to-day life, but that is not the purpose of this question. I used to give you examples of what I meant and why I was asking. Even from a young age, you always understood what I was doing, but I still think it's good to explain it occasionally.

3. CONSTANTLY REASSURE HIM THAT HE CAN TRUST YOU.

Without trust, this lesson is pointless. It actually goes back to the lesson on always doing what you say you're going to do. If your son trusts you with little things, then he is likely to trust you with more intimate things. I used to say, "If you ever want to talk to me about something, but maybe you are embarrassed or shy or confused, just know that you can trust me to keep a secret. Do you trust me?" But of course, you can't force trust. It must be earned over a lifetime.

4. DON'T BE ANNOYING, BUT ASK IT CONSISTENTLY.

There is, of course, no perfectly right or wrong way to do this. It's not an absolute truth. Your opinion or situation may be different from mine. But in my opinion, you should not ask this question too often or it can become annoying. I learned this the hard way with you. I used to ask you this almost every night at bedtime. One night you finally said, "Dad, please stop asking me that." At first it hurt my feelings, but then I realized that you were right. The question didn't mean anything special because I asked it too much. But it is important to be consistent. I think about once or twice a month is plenty. But again, you do what you think is best.

5. SOMETIMES IT HELPS TO BE SPECIFIC WITH CERTAIN ISSUES OR SITUATIONS.

Don't get me wrong, the whole purpose of this question is for it to be open-ended and vague. But sometimes it can be beneficial to be more direct and specific, depending on what might be going on in life. For example, from time to time when you were younger, I would talk to you about why no one should ever touch your private areas. Then I would directly ask if anyone ever has.

Another example is the night you gave your life to Christ. I asked if there was anything you wanted to talk about, but you said no. We had been talking about Jesus, sin, and salvation for many months, so I got a bit more specific. I said, "Have you been thinking more about Jesus? Is there anything that you want to discuss about him?"

It was almost as if you had been waiting for me to ask because you instantly said, "Yes, I want to ask him into my heart. Can you help me?" It was one of the best nights of my life. Being specific in this situation was important.

6. START YOUNG.

It's important to create this special time from an early age. The obvious reason is that's when trust is initially created. If you decide not to use this question when Noah is young for whatever reason, I would recommend that you still try to start using it when he gets older. But it will be more difficult. Older teenagers can sometimes think that their parents are trying to probe too much, or find out about their personal lives. But if you start this process as a young child, then it will become normal and expected.

7. DON'T GET FRUSTRATED WHEN HE SAYS NO.

Let me go ahead and burst your bubble. As much as Noah is going to love you and trust you, he will still say no many times. In fact, he will likely say that he has nothing to talk about way more often than he does. But this is a good thing. It's OK that these special, private talks are rare. That's actually what makes them so wonderful. So don't get frustrated. You never want to him to think that he should just make something up in order to please you. This question is not about you; it's about him.

8. FINALLY, DON'T OVERACT NO MATTER WHAT HE SAYS.

Remember, the whole purpose of this question is to get your son to trust you and talk to you about personal or private issues. Especially as he gets older, some of these issues can be deep. Teenagers are faced with too many things that are way too big for their undeveloped minds to understand. So when he asks you or tells you something that may sound shocking, don't overreact. The worst thing you can do is to make him feel humiliated or regretful. Trust and open communication takes years to build, but seconds to destroy. As the Bible says in James 1:19, "Be quick to listen, slow to speak, and slow to become angry."

CHAPTER 13

LESSON 10: PLEASE FORGIVE ME

DAVID, LET ME teach you three little words that have the potential to create more respect for you from your children then you can imagine. And, no, they are not "I love you." If, as a father, you can learn to use the phrase "please forgive me," then you have just elevated yourself to an elite level of parenting. And by the way, there is a huge substantive different between "I'm sorry," and "please forgive me."

The Bible says in Matthew 5:23–24, *"Therefore if you are presenting your offering at the altar, and there remember that your brother has something against you, leave your offering there before the altar and go; first be reconciled to your brother, and then come and present your offering."* If we, as Christians, should react this way to our "brothers" or friends, then how much more should we apply this truth to our own kids? Parenting is difficult. There is no doubt that every mother and father has done or said things at times that they regretted. Kids don't need perfect parents, but they do need parents who admit their mistakes and try to make them right.

Here's the bottom line, David: if you do or say something wrong as a dad, then don't just apologize to your son; ask for his forgiveness. And by the way, this requires a massive amount of humility. But think of the incredible lessons that it teaches. Now of course there are times when saying you're sorry is appropriate.

"I'm sorry I was late."

"I'm sorry I accidentally broke your toy."

"I'm sorry I can't make it to your game tonight."

But this lesson is way beyond simply apologizing for mistakes or accidents. What I'm talking about, David, is when we as fathers sin, or act inappropriately or disrespectfully, then we need to use this bad example as a teachable moment. And you accomplish this by asking your child to forgive you. Think about it from a kid's perspective. Their whole lives are all about parents and other adults telling them what to do and punishing them when they mess up. They quickly learn lessons about consequences, good decisions, discipline, and conduct. Most kids even learn how to say, "I'm sorry." But one very powerful foundational lesson that can often be neglected by parents is the importance of forgiveness.

I can vividly recall when the value of this lesson was revealed to me. You were seven years old. I was having a bad day, and I took it out on you. You were throwing rocks in the yard and you accidentally hit my car and scratched it. You immediately came and confessed to me, but regretfully I lost my cool. I called you a name, spanked you harder than normal, screamed at you way beyond what you deserved, and then sent you to your room. After a few minutes, I calmed down and instantly felt ashamed at how poorly I treated you. First of all, I don't believe you should ever call your child a derogatory name. And secondly, I was way out of line, and I set a terrible example to you on how to handle bad situations. When I walked in your room, you were sitting on your bed, crying. I can still see your face in my mind. I knew that just saying sorry wasn't enough. So I knelt down beside your bed, grabbed your hands, and said, "David, I am so sorry for how I just treated you. I should never have called you a name, and I overreacted. Daddy messes up sometimes just like everyone else. Will you please forgive me?"

The reason this lesson on forgiveness is so important is because it gives the child all of the power. Kids are used to being told what to do, how to do it, and when to do it. There are very few times in the life of a child where he has any power or authority whatsoever. When you humble yourself as a father and ask your child to forgive you, you are literally giving him temporary power over you. Trust me, these will be memorable moments for your kids. And again, it presents a teachable moment. Now you have accomplished two great things. First, you have displayed a humble spirit and set a good example by admitting you were wrong and asking for forgiveness. But second, now you can help teach your son what it means to forgive someone and why it's important.

Mark 11:25 says, *"Whenever you are praying, if you are holding anything against anyone, forgive him, so that your Father who is in heaven will also forgive you your sins."* Jesus not only teaches his children to ask for forgiveness when we are at fault, but he also commands us to forgive those who have wronged us. There are few things more dangerous to the soul of a believer than holding on to bitterness or anger. David, can you see why this is such a powerful lesson to instill in Noah? When parents ask their kids to forgive them, we can then turn a bad situation into a good situation by teaching this incredible lesson. You are literally giving your child the choice to either forgive you or to hold on to a grudge. You are not making the statement, "Forgive me." Even that sounds like another command from a parent to a child. Instead you are humbly asking, "Will you forgive me?"

And when your child agrees to offer you forgiveness, now you, the father, can point to The Father. You can talk about God sending his son Jesus to die on the cross for sins. You can explain how Jesus forgives our sins even though we don't deserve it. And now you have a practical situation that he will understand. He didn't just hear about forgiveness; he experienced it. How cool would it be for you to end this moment by opening the Bible and reading Ephesians 4:32 together? *"Be kind and compassionate to one another, forgiving each other, just as Christ forgave you."*

CHAPTER 14

LESSON 11: TEACH MONEY LESSONS

THERE ARE MANY things that your mother and I may have failed at as parents, but teaching you to be wise with money was not one of them. I am so proud of you for being a good steward of the money that God has entrusted to you. You know more about money as a young adult then most men do as senior adults. Between the lessons that I have taught you, the financial books you've read, and the Dave Ramsey classes that you and Hailey have taken, I am confident that you are prepared to live an abundant life.

But it's not only important what you know; it's equally important what you teach your kids. Now that you are going to be a father, it's your turn to instill wise money lessons in Noah. The twenty-five lessons that I'm giving you are not in any order of importance. The only exception is that building a strong biblical foundation is of the utmost importance. Other than that, the rest of these lessons are probably equal in value. With that said, this lesson on teaching money lessons at home may do more good and prevent more harm than any of the others. Some of my parenting lessons are simply ideas; you can take them, leave them, apply them, or change them. But I'm telling you, son, do not neglect this one.

I have thought long and hard about exactly what I want to say to you about this. The topic of money is such a large and general topic. You could read a dozen books about money and still have much to learn. But after much prayer, I believe that God has revealed to me what he wants me to leave to my son and grandson. This lesson is extremely practical and basic. No theory or fluff, only meat and potatoes.

So here's the bottom line, David: You need to teach your kids about money, or someone else will. Culture has so much to say about finances and most of it is dangerous. I promise you, Noah will learn about money from friends, teachers, TV shows, social media, books. and a variety of other sources. You need a strategy. You need to teach him what the Bible says about money. You need to show him what it means to be a wise steward. You need to model self-control. You need to let him experience the joy of giving. You need to explain the value of saving and investing. Many fathers understand money, but few teach it to their kids. Be countercultural, son.

Money should be a regular part of conversations at home. Some families think it's rude to talk about money; I think it's dangerous not to. We started teaching you about money when you were only four or five years old. You remember, right? We used another lesson called the power of repetition to engrave into your mind a few truths about money that we wanted you to know. As you got older, of course, we taught you deeper truths and more specific lessons. So what I want to give you are a few money lessons to teach your kids when they are young, and a few more to teach as they get older.

AS A KID (5-10 YEARS OLD)

When Noah is old enough to have meaningful conversations, that's when you should start teaching him money lessons. That's what we did with you, and it worked. There are four important things that I want you to know about teaching your son about money when he is still young. First, repetition is key. Kids can become masters of anything if they start young enough and repeat it enough times. When you teach him money lessons at this age, it's important that you repeat them over and over. When I started teaching you the lessons that I'm about to list, I made you repeat them to me at least once or twice a week, without exception.

Second, the main goal at this young age is simply to develop money consciousness. You are not trying to create a miniature Dave Ramsey or inspire him to become a financial planner. Your job is to help him learn about money; how it works; why it's important; what it does for people; how to use it wisely; etc. One of the great travesties of this generation is seeing how many college students and young adults have no concept of money whatsoever. They may know how to spend it, but very few are money conscious.

The third thing that is important is for Noah to learn the value of a dollar. Many kids don't know the true difference between one hundred dollars and one thousand dollars. It's just a big number. But when we teach our kids how to handle money, how to spend it, how to save it, and how to give it, they can quickly understand its true value.

Fourth and finally, keep it simple. Remember when your son is five or eight years old, the only lessons that he will remember long term are simple lessons.

There are many great money lessons that fathers can teach their sons when they are young, but here are the main ones that I hope you will pass on. I call it: The 4 Money Rules. It's catchy and easy to remember.

#1-Work Hard, Get Paid
#2-Always Save Some
#3-Tithe
#4-Debt Is Bad

It's not important that a five-year-old and explain in detail why debt can be so dangerous for families. All that matters is that he subconsciously accepts the fact that debt is a bad thing. It's also not important that a six-year-old tithes exactly 10 percent of his income (chores) on a weekly or monthly basis. All that matters is that he learns to start giving some of his earned money to the church. It's not important that a seven-year-old fully understands compound interest. All that matters is that he creates the discipline of setting aside money to save for later. It's not important that an eight-year-old gets a paycheck or learns to balance a checkbook. All that matters is that he equates hard work with payment. Every day immediately after you completed your chores, we paid you for your work. We didn't believe in giving an allowance. We taught you to work for your money. If you work, you get paid. If you don't work, you don't get paid, period.

AS A TEENAGER (11-18 YEARS OLD)

Teenagers can handle more than many adults give them credit for. As a youth minister, you know this to be true. Teenagers are certainly immature and irresponsible, but their capacity to learn and comprehend information might be more impressive than it is for adults. During these moldable years, it is important for you to teach money lessons on a deeper level. Now you can move beyond the "what" (the lesson) and start to explain the "why" and "how."

Teenagers will not practice and appreciate all of these money lessons as early teens (eleven to fourteen), but in their later teenage years (fifteen to eighteen), it will become second nature for them. Remember, you are teaching your child at the core. It's way bigger than what he knows; it's about who he is. But these lessons on money must be taught *and* caught. You must first model the lesson yourself, and then look for opportunities and teachable moments to further drive home your point. One example that comes to mind is when you bought your first car. Your mother and I told you for years that we were not going to buy it for you, so you needed to save money and make temporary sacrifices. When you turned sixteen you didn't have enough money, so you asked us to help you. We lovingly reminded you of many of the times when you decided to spend money on stuff you didn't need, instead of saving for your car. As a result, it took you ten more months of hard work and frivolous saving before you had enough money for the car. Lesson learned.

These money lessons that I hope you teach Noah as a teenager are not a complete list. You will certainly want to add your own. The whole point, though, is for you to model and teach wise money lessons in order to prepare your son for the real world. I'm not going to give you much detail to these lessons because you already know what they mean. I just want your mind focused on how you can help Noah to start understanding money. Here are a few important money lessons for your teenager.

1. The borrower is slave to the lender.
    Proverbs 22:7 says, *"The rich rule over the poor, and the borrower is servant to the lender."*

2. The more you give, the more likely you are to receive.
    Proverbs 11:24–25 says, *"One man gives freely, yet gains even more; another withholds unduly, but comes to poverty. A generous man will prosper; he who refreshes others will himself be refreshed."*

3. If you are not content and thankful, then you can have everything and yet have nothing.
    Philippians 4:12 says, *"I know what it is to be in need, and I know what it is to have plenty. I have learned the secret of being content in any and every situation."*

4. Anyone can become wealthy over time.
    Some people can obtain wealth in a few years, while it may take others forty years. But anyone can become wealthy over time if he is wise with his money.

5. Don't focus on "can" you afford something, but rather "should" you buy it.
    Teach him how to show self-control. Help him to reason through if he should buy something, even though he has enough money.

6. Don't try to keep up with the Joneses.
    This bad philosophy creates a viscous cycle of debt, materialism, and eventually marriage problems. There is nothing wrong with buying nice things if you can afford them. But if opinions of others influence purchases, then it's not a money issue; it's a heart issue.

7. Clearly identify wants vs. needs.
    Every teenager needs this lesson. Help your son to realize the difference between wants and needs, and then teach him to categorize his potential purchases accordingly.

8. When you want to make a big purchase, it's wise to sleep on it first.

    This is not an absolute truth, but it will teach him self-control and more importantly, how to avoid making emotional purchases that are often followed by regret.

9. Pay yourself first.

    Teenagers must learn to set aside money every month or from every paycheck. Learning and applying this lesson early in life could literally be the difference between millions of dollars over his lifetime.

10. A credit card is like a pet snake. When kept under control, it's no harm, but is it really worth the risk?

    From the moment a young man steps out of his home and onto the college campus, he is attacked with opportunities for credit cards. Credit cards can devastate a young person who doesn't know how to use them. But since you will prepare Noah for the potential dangers that credit cards can create, he will be able to resist.

CHAPTER 15

LESSON 12: THE IMPORTANCE OF WORK ETHIC

DAVID, THIS IS one of those lessons where the title says it all. In fact, this will likely be the shortest lesson that I have for you for two reasons. One, because I raised you to have an extremely hard work ethic, so I know that you already have this one down. But second because I can say only so much about this topic in a few sentences. The bottom line is: teach your kids to work hard, period.

> Proverbs 14:23 says, *"All hard work brings a profit, but mere talk leads only to poverty."*
> Proverbs 10:4 says, *"Lazy hands make a man poor, but diligent hands bring wealth."*

Work ethic is more than a lesson to teach; it's a principle to instill. Instill in Noah's heart the value and importance of a hard work ethic. And it's a good thing that you will have Noah in your home for eighteen years because it will take every bit of that to accomplish this goal. That's why I say that there's only so much I can say in a few words.

There are few things that sadden me at this stage of my life than to see a lazy young man. Sad might be the wrong word. It makes me angry. It makes me angry with his parents for not doing a better job, and it makes me angry because he may possibly end up living off the support of the government—in other words, our tax dollars. But we can't fix other people. All you can do is work hard yourself, set a good example to others, and raise your kids to have the same work ethic.

The only thing that I really want to say to you, David, is to teach and demand a strong work ethic in everything Noah does. This principle isn't just about doing chores and eventually getting a job. That's the mistake many parents make. They confine work ethic only to a job. So kids grow up to become lazy adults who work hard from nine to five. This principle applies to all areas, to everything he touches. Ecclesiastes 9:10 says, *"Whatever your hand finds to do, do it with all your might."*

I love this verse. Solomon says that we should work hard at everything we do, no matter what it is. Teach this important principle to Noah. It will literally take you eighteen years to accomplish, but stick to it. When you tell him to clean up after himself as a little boy, but he doesn't get it all, don't finish the job for him, just encourage him to keep going until it's done. When he makes his bed, but it looks worse than when he started, don't applaud him for giving a halfhearted effort; rather, show him how to do it better, then let him improve. When it comes to schoolwork, don't demand straight As or perfect grades; rather, demand hard work. If he studies hard, but gets a B, reward his hard work. If he gives a last-minute effort to finish a school project that he kept putting off, and he gets a bad grade, don't punish the grade; rather, punish his laziness. In sports, it's not important that he makes twenty points or gets two hits or scores the winning goal. What's important is that he works hard to get ready for the game, and that he gives 100 percent of his effort during the game. It's that little thing called hustle.

Of course work ethic does also apply to a job or career. But teach your son that he doesn't have to be the smartest, or the best looking, or the most outgoing to become successful. Instead, he must work harder. Help him to understand that a strong work ethic levels the playing field. Noah can get ahead, beat out the competition, and earn promotions by outworking everyone else. No need for sucking up to the boss. No need to cheat. No need to step on anyone else. Just work harder.

I'm so proud of your work ethic, son. You worked hard as a kid with your chores and homework. You worked hard in sports. You worked hard in college. You worked hard in seminary. You work hard now in ministry. Now pay this lesson forward. Raise hard-working kids. You can't control the next generation, but you can control your family.

CHAPTER 16

LESSON 13: THE THANKFUL BENCH

I WANT TO share one of my favorite verses with you, David. It is one that you know all too well because we had you memorize it as a young child. In fact, you repeated this verse to us dozens of times throughout your adolescent years. It is one of the foundational verses that God gave us to raise you with. 1 Thessalonians 5:16–18 says, *"Be joyful always; pray continually; give thanks in all circumstances, for this is God's will for you in Christ Jesus."*

One of the most dangerous words in our culture today is *entitlement*. Teenagers and young adults are infected with this disease. Entitlement is the belief that a person inherently deserves privileges or special treatment. I know that you have experienced this mentality personally in student ministry. But I promise you, entitlement is just as prevalent in many young adults as it is in teenagers.

The only way I know to combat this entitlement mentality is with a grateful heart. Teach your son to be thankful, David. He likely won't learn it anywhere else, so teach it at home. Make humility, gratitude, and thanksgiving the cornerstones of your home. You will not be a perfect parent, and your children won't be perfect, either. But do not slack off in this area. Our culture has enough arrogant men full of entitlement. It needs more humble men full of gratitude. The good news is that it's your choice; which do you want Noah to become?

Let's talk about the "thankful bench." I know that you remember it from childhood, but allow me to explain it the best I can. The "thankful bench" was a literal bench that sat in our front yard. One day you and I were sitting on the bench talking about who knows what, and then I asked you, "Hey, buddy, we are so blessed, aren't we? What are you thankful for?" You listed a few things, and so did I. Sometime later we were sitting there again, and I asked you the same question. Suddenly, we not only had a tradition, but we had more teachable moments. We called it the "thankful bench," and we made it a regular routine to sit out there and take turns discussing what we were so grateful for and how God had so blessed our family.

But I quickly found a second purpose for the "thankful bench." Whenever you needed an attitude adjustment, or you were going through a period of selfishness, we visited the bench. Sometimes you loved it, and other times you were annoyed. But that never stopped us from sharing our gratitude and creating some special moments. But as you know, David, it's not about the bench. Rather, it's about the mind-set that it creates in a moldable young boy. It's about the realization of how blessed we truly are.

The "thankful bench" is a metaphor for living in a perpetual state of gratitude. This is the lesson that I want you to pass on. Teach Noah to be thankful in the little things in life, not just the big ones. Teach him to be humble before all people. Teach him to be grateful to the people who serve and provide for him. Teach him that he is no better than anyone else, and no one is better than him, either. Teach him that no one owes him anything. Teach him that entitlement is a sin.

Instilling gratitude in a child takes years. Create your own moments and opportunities with him. Maybe you could even have your own "thankful bench." Whether you use a literal bench, or a sofa, or a bed, or a rock, it doesn't really matter. The point is to have a special place where you discuss and teach gratitude, and where your children can be reminded of how blessed they are. But this lesson must also take place beyond the bench. It must be constant and never-ending. Remember, gratitude is more than a trait; it's a lifestyle.

Here are just a few examples of how to constantly model and train your child to be thankful.

- Randomly ask: "What are you thankful for?" You don't need a purpose or special occasion.
- At dinner: Teach the kids to thank the cook. If Hailey cooks, then you be the first to thank her. Then tell Noah to do the same.
- After special occasions: When you do something fun, like go on a trip or vacation, on the way home, discuss in the car how blessed you are.
- Nightly prayers: Thank God for the things that we often take for granted. Be specific. Thank God for healthy legs and arms to be able to play sports, or for eyes and ears to be able to enjoy nature.
- After leaving relatives: Talk about how thankful you are for family, grandparents, relatives, etc.
- Schoolteachers, coaches, and church leaders: Teach your kids to thank them for their time and servant hearts. You, as the parent, need to do the same.
- Punishments: This is a great way to punish a younger kid for having a poor attitude or for behaving badly. Make him right a list of twenty things he is thankful for. As he is writing this list, I promise his mood will change.

CHAPTER 17

LESSON 14: SUCCESS MOTTOS

You REMEMBER THE good ole success mottos, don't you, David? Of course you do. I've actually kept them all these years, and I want you to have them. They are included in this final gift for you. By now you have probably already seen them. Even though we have had this discussion numerous times, I want to take this last opportunity to explain what they were all about, why we did them, and more importantly, why I hope you pass them on to Noah.

First and foremost, these success mottos have never been about financial gain. Success is not defined by a bank account. I have always desired for you to become financially free, but certainly no dollar amount equates success, at least in my mind.

Second, I want to remind you how we used them. You don't have to do it this exact way, but it was fun for us. Each week I found a success motto either in the Bible, in a book that I was reading, or from a life lesson that I wanted to pass on to you. I wrote it on a three-by-five index card. At the top I wrote "Success Mottos" and then put the actual motto or quote under it. One example is: "No man ever became great except by going through many great mistakes." I then put the card on your bathroom mirror for you to read every day as you brushed your teeth. I changed the card out with a new one each week.

Third, allow me to clearly explain why we started doing this, and why we kept it up for over ten years. One day when you were a young child, I was reading a book by Jack Canfield called *The Success Principles*. While reading that book, I had a sudden epiphany: Success is a mind-set. If my son is going to be successful, then I need to fill his mind and heart with positive, wise, life-giving messages. When this thought came to me, I suddenly became aware of what kinds of messages our culture was feeding you. The key word, David, is *aware*. No loving parent tries to fill their child's mind with negative or damaging thoughts. But many parents simply are not aware of it. I want you to not only become aware of these messages that society will feed your son, but then to fight them with success mottos.

Here are just a fraction of the types of mental messages that kids hear daily:

You aren't good enough.
You are too ugly, fat, short, etc.
You will never amount to anything.
Rich people are bad.
No one loves you.
You are stupid.
You will always be poor.
You don't have any friends.
Blame someone else for your mistakes.
You are entitled to more or better.
You might as well quit or give up.
I was just born this way.
I am a loser.
If someone wrongs you, get even.
Don't trust anyone.
Don't accept responsibility for your choices.

These messages can be devastating to children and teenagers. So, as a father, you must fight these negative lies with positive truths. And the two best ways to accomplish this are by feeding your child Scripture and success mottos. First, let's look at a few passages. What does God have to say about the power of our own thoughts?

- Matthew 15:11: *"It's not what goes into the mouth that defiles a person, but what comes out of the mouth that defiles him."* The mind will often accept what the mouth speaks. It is so important to teach your child to speak positive words. We can all be negative and hard on ourselves. But when you hear them from your child, you must quickly correct them. Don't allow him to say things like: "I'm not good enough," "I'll never make it," "I hate him," or "Everyone is against me." The more he says them, the more his mind will believe them.

- Romans 12:2: *"Be transformed by the renewing of your mind."* I love this verse because God puts the responsibility on us to change our thinking. From time to time, your son will also need a renewing of his mind or attitude. Explain to him that we tend to become that which we think about the most. Teach him how to think in terms of success and blessing, not failure or lacking.

- Philippians 4:8: *"Whatever is true, whatever is noble, whatever is right, whatever is pure, whatever is lovely, whatever is admirable—if anything is excellent or praiseworthy—think about such things."* This, David, is why Scripture and success mottos are so valuable. They constantly fill your child's mind with positive thoughts. When kids fill their minds with junk music, junk TV shows, junk social media, and junk friends, what do you think they are going to produce—junk.

Finally, son, I want to leave you with a few specific truths that I want my grandson to know. Since I won't be there to tell him these things, I need you to do it buddy. This is certainly not a complete list, nor are these absolute truths. These are simply my opinions of what I tried to instill in you, and what I hope that you will pass on. Do you remember these success mottos?

- *God made you awesome.*
- *Honesty is the most import virtue. Without honesty, nothing else matters.*

- *Accepting responsibility for your actions is one of the hardest of all self-disciplines.*
- *Never settle for less than God's best for your life.*
- *Self-discipline is the most important element to success in life.*
- *Your greatest obstacle in life will be conquering and mastering yourself.*
- *There is nothing more powerful than your mind. Whatever you think about, that's what you will become.*
- *Life is best lived in service to others.*
- *To experience great things, you must take great risks.*
- *Your integrity is the one thing that only you can control.*
- *If you can't forgive people when they hurt you, how can you ever expect to be forgiven?*
- *No one is born with a work ethic. Hard work is something that you must learn to do.*

CHAPTER 18

LESSON 15: THE FORBIDDEN PHRASE

I LIKE TO think that you had a great upbringing, David. Our home was full of love, forgiveness, grace, and honesty. We had so much fun together. I believe that one of the reasons that we all got along so well is because everyone understood what was expected, allowed, and forbidden. In our household there were some things that you just didn't do. They were not gray areas, and there was no wiggle room. You didn't talk back. You didn't roll your eyes. You didn't take the Lord's name in vain. You didn't use profanity. You didn't scream. And you never used the forbidden phrase.

You know exactly what I'm referring to, don't you? In fact, we called it "the forbidden phrase." The one phrase that you, your mother, and I were not allowed to use was: *That's not fair!* You and I have had this conversation dozens of times, so I know that you understand why I am so adamant about this. But for Noah's sake, please allow me to opine.

David, I believe that this is one of the most dangerous phrases there is. Actually, it's not the words themselves that concern me, but it's the root issue that lies underneath. When you were younger, we used to have conversations about this all of the time. You didn't really understand why it was bad or why it made me so upset. You just didn't want to get in trouble so you said, "Yes, sir." Even now as a grown man, you may be reading this lesson, wondering if you are even going to share it with your kids. Whether you do or not is up to you. All I want is for you to become a great father and raise Noah to be a godly young man. And I believe with all of my heart that this lesson is vital to his future growth.

This lesson has become all the more real to me over the last few months. This cancer is literally killing me one slow day at a time. As I'm writing these very words, I have tears in my eyes. My heart is broken at the thought of possibly never meeting my grandson. It hurts too much to even think about no longer having our Sunday night phone calls. And I can't properly describe how devastated I am to be leaving my bride behind. I could very easily and justifiably throw my hands up and shout, "It's not fair." But what good would that do, David? All it would do is cause me to feel sorry for myself. But instead I choose to be thankful for these last days. I'm thankful for the opportunity and the strength to be able to write down these twenty-five lessons for you.

I want to share with you why this phrase is so dangerous. I want you to know why I was so strict about it. I want you forbid this phrase from your house as well. And as you do, this is what I want you to teach Noah.

1. **Life isn't fair.** Nowhere in Scripture does God say that life is fair and everything is going to work out perfectly. In fact, life can be brutal. Bad things do happen to good people. Sometimes good things happen to people who deserve bad things, and bad things happen to people who deserve good things. We can try our best to figure it out, but that's just the way it is. We are all sinners, and we live in a sinful world. Life isn't fair.

2. **The phrase "that's not fair" creates a victim mentality.** This is the main reason that your mother and I didn't allow this phrase. There were no victims in our family, only victors. We raised you to take charge of your life and make the most of it. Too many adults live with this victim mentality. They think that bad things happen to them, people are out to get them, and nothing is their fault. I can't imagine how depressing it must be to live like this.

3. **Promote personal responsibility.** What's important is how we respond to that which "isn't fair." Since bad or unfortunate things happen to all people, the only difference between two people is how they choose to respond. Teach your kids to be in

control. Kids and teenagers love the idea of being in charge. I used to say to you, "David, you are in charge here. Only you can decide how you respond to this situation." Take the focus off the unfair situation and place it on the decision to respond with courage and optimism.

And now for the difficult part, David. When you say that something is forbidden in your family, you must back it up with consistency. It's not something that you can let slip by from time to time. There's a difference between discouraging this phrase and forbidding it. Be strong with your conviction on this. Noah doesn't always have to understand the *why* as long as he obeys the *what*. He needs to know that this is very important. So when he is young, of course, you will need to be patient with him as he is learning. But as he gets older, be firm. When you were elementary age, I used to say things like, "Hey, buddy, I don't want you to say that's not fair, OK?" But after about age ten or so it was more like, "David, you know better; don't use that phrase."

Please allow this old man to say two more things. First, you must patiently and specifically explain to him why this phrase is forbidden. This is not one of those "do as I say" moments. We are not trying to raise obedient robots; we're trying to raise godly young men. So explain some of the points that I listed. Repeat it a thousand times if necessary. Ask him if he understands. This lesson is completely countercultural. Everywhere you turn people use this phrase and live as victims. So be patient as you help him understand why it's so dangerous.

And the last thing I want to say is to be mindful of your own language and attitude. As difficult as it can be, you and Hailey need to model this lesson if you are going to teach it. You must remove this phrase from your vocabulary. If Noah hears you say, "That's not fair," or perceives that you have a victim mind-set, then it will be very difficult for him to learn this lesson. This lesson is both taught and caught. You will never be a perfect parent, but please be aware of your words. Little ears are always listening.

CHAPTER 19

LESSON 16: DEVELOP HIS LEADERSHIP SKILLS

ONE OF MY favorite verses in the Bible is 1 Timothy 4:12. It says, *"Don't let anyone look down on you because you are young, but set an example for the believers in speech, in life, in love, in faith, and in purity."* I not only love the meaning of the passage, but the context as well. The apostle Paul is writing this letter to his younger protégé, Timothy. Paul is mentoring him in the ministry and teaching him how to lead his people by example. Anyone can preach a few good words, but Paul encourages Timothy to also lead others with his lifestyle. Timothy was younger than many of his followers, especially the elders. But Paul tells him that his age is irrelevant, that people are watching him, and that other believers need a model to follow.

Leadership has always been important to me. I tried my best to instill leadership qualities in you, also. As I come to the conclusion of my life, one of my proudest achievements has been watching you continue to grow and develop into a much better leader than I ever was. I'm so proud of you. But please understand, David, that you are not a great leader today simply because you are a minister and in a leadership position in a church. Leadership has nothing to do with position. You are a great leader because we have worked very hard to develop your leadership skills throughout your entire life. And this is exactly what you should do with Noah. Don't just hope that he becomes a good leader one day; rather, you need to develop him into a great leader.

I want to give you some leadership development tips. Some of these worked really well for us, and many others I have learned along the way. But first and foremost, the best way I know to develop young leaders is to simply give them opportunities to lead. Leadership is best learned on the go; it's on-the-job training. So this lesson is a bit different than the others. It's not just about you teaching Noah with words or giving him some father/son talks. In order to properly develop his leadership skills you must give him opportunities to lead, encourage him to make decisions, allow him to fail, and then help him to learn.

Like all of the other lessons, this is not a complete list, nor is it absolute truth. These are simply some tips to guide you. So here is some fatherly advice on how to develop leadership skills in the life of your son.

1. ALLOW HIM TO MAKE CHOICES.

Children and teenagers go through most of their adolescent lives being told what to do, when to do it, and how to do it better. This is exactly how it should be, but from time to time we need to shake things up. One of the best qualities of a good leader is decisiveness. A leader has the ability to gather information and then make a definitive decision without second-guessing himself. In order for him to develop this skill, you must first give your son opportunities to make his own decisions. This can be hard because the parent usually knows what's best for him, even if he doesn't. David, I'm obviously not suggesting that you let your son live his life however he wants. I simply mean to thoughtfully and strategically give him the chance to make his own decisions. He will feel empowered and appreciate your trust in him. But most importantly, this will give you another teachable moment. It's your job to use discernment with this freedom. If he is consistently making poor decisions, then take that freedom from him and show him why he is not ready. But if he starts to make wise decisions, then give him more chances with even more important ramifications.

2. HELP HIM TO LEARN THROUGH MISTAKES.

When kids make mistakes, parents often times rush to correct the mistake and then punish the behavior. This is natural, but it doesn't teach leadership skills. David, as you will find, one of the hardest things for a parent is to allow children to make mistakes, especially when you know what's best for them. But sometimes we must let go, just a bit, and allow him to make his own mistakes. But here's the key, David. This is only beneficial if we then help him to learn through the mistake. This is the part that many parents miss.

The best way that I have found to accomplish this is by teaching him to weigh the pros and cons of a decision. Once he understands how to do this and why, then you need to give him a chance to exercise this knowledge. When he makes a good decision, celebrate it. But when he makes a bad decision, show him how to learn from it. Teach him that all great leaders make mistakes. The difference between good leaders and great leaders is that some learn to fail forward. Don't make the mistake of getting upset and giving him an "I told you so" speech. Instead, talk through the mistake. Ask him what he learned, what he would do differently, and if he accurately weighed the pros and cons or if he just made a decision on instant gratification. These will be some fun learning opportunities.

3. TEACH HIM TO REMAIN HUMBLE.

Philippians 2:3 says, *"Do nothing out of selfish ambition or vain conceit, but in humility consider others better than yourself."* In our culture today, arrogance and self-promotion are the norm. Most of the celebrities, actors, athletes, and musicians that kids see online or on TV are all about themselves. Because of this, parents must work extra hard to teach humility. Because of our sinful nature, humans are at the core very selfish and self-serving. Humility is not natural, and very few people are born with this trait. Rather, humility is a learned behavior.

Teach your son to be humble. Explain over and over again what this means and what it looks like. You, of course, must model humility in your home. If he excels in school, celebrate his grades, but then bring him back down, lest he becomes arrogant. If he excels in sports, celebrate his accomplishments, but then bring him back down, lest he becomes cocky. If he excels in any of the arts, celebrate his creativity, but then bring him back down, lest he become conceited. I remember a time when you made the middle school basketball team and you let it go to your head. You allowed yourself to believe that you were hot stuff. You stopped hanging out with some of your long-time friends who didn't make the team. Do you remember that? Even the best of people need a dose of humility from time to time. Your mother and I gladly gave it to you by giving the choice to either change your attitude, or quit the team. Needless to say, you came back to your old self rather quickly. Again, humility is unnatural; so when these moments of ego arise, and they will, don't get upset. This, too, is a teachable moment. Just take him to John 13 and show him the ultimate model of humility found in Jesus.

4. FORCE HIM TO PRACTICE PROBLEM SOLVING.

Good leaders are good problem solvers. But the only way to become good in this area is through experience. The natural instinct for a parent when a problem arises for their child is to solve it for them. It's an act of love, no doubt. But if you want your son to become a great leader, he must learn how to solve his own problems. Your job is to manage this with discernment. If you feel that he is up to the challenge, then allow him the chance to figure out a solution to his own problems. Coach him through it. Tell him that you trust him to use wisdom and patience and to do the right thing. The best way to help him without solving the issue for him is by asking thought-provoking questions. My favorite question to ask is one that I learned from Pastor Andy Stanley. Ask: What is the wise thing to do?

5. WARN HIM ABOUT ALWAYS FOLLOWING THE CROWD.

Negative peer pressure is one of the most difficult issues that your child will ever face. It's very hard to say no to what everyone else is doing.

Leaders are not impervious to peer pressure, but they are certainly aware of it and they fight hard against it. Leaders do what's right, not what's popular. Exodus 23:2 says, *"Do not follow the crowd in doing wrong."* Teach Noah that it is not only OK to go against the crowd, but it's actually encouraged.

6. SHOW HIM HOW TO BE A SERVANT-LEADER.

Teach your son that the evidence of a great leader isn't found in how many people are serving him, but in how many people he is serving. In Mark 10:43–44 Jesus says, *"Whoever wants to become great among you must be your servant, and whoever wants to be first must be slave of all."* Some people are born with a servant heart or a care-giving mind-set. But many people are not. So be careful not to get too frustrated if Noah is in the latter category. The Bible says that no one has all of the gifts.

What's important is not what comes naturally, but what he chooses to do. Leaders choose to serve. But you must show him how. Don't make the mistake of just telling him to serve others while you sit back and watch. Serve together. Say things like: "Come on, buddy let's go help clean up the kitchen." Or, "Let's go help the coach put all of the gear up." Or, "How can we serve your teacher for being so nice to you?"

7. EXPECT GOOD COMMUNICATION.

Leaders don't have to be great public speakers, but they must learn to communicate effectively. This has nothing to do with being an extravert or Type A personality. In fact, you were extremely introverted until high school. But regardless of your naturally shy personality, I always taught you to communicate well. You had to look people in the eyes, speak up, and talk clearly. The best way to teach good communication is by forcing it. Here are a few examples. When an adult asks your child a question, don't answer for him; make him do it. When a waiter is taking your food order, make your son order his own meal. When you go visit relatives, make him tell people what's been going on in his life. If he needs to miss baseball practice, make him go tell the coach. If he wants a friend to come over and play, make him call the friend's parent and ask for permission. The point of this is not to embarrass your child. Never do that. The purpose is to help him to become an effective communicator over time.

8. POINT OUT REAL LIFE EXAMPLES OF LEADERSHIP.

This one is simple. When you see examples of good leadership, point them out. Kids can identify better with real-life scenarios than they can with theoretical lessons. So let others do your teaching for you, but you must be aware enough to point them out. Again, ask questions. Who is the best leader you know? Which character in that movie do you think was a good leader? Which leadership qualities do you like in that person from the book you're reading?

9. USE THE WORD "LEADER" ALL OF THE TIME.

Trust me, at times you will feel like you are the most annoying dad in the world. But it is your job to develop his leadership skills, no one else's. And he needs your help. I used to use the word "leader" with you so much that even your mother would get frustrated. I wouldn't just say that you need to be early for practice; rather, I would say leaders are early for practice. I wouldn't say do the right thing; I would say leaders do the right thing. Leader are honest. Leaders don't wait for others to decide. Leaders don't disrespect their teacher. Leaders help protect those in need. You get the idea.

10. ACKNOWLEDGE AND REWARD ACTS OF LEADERSHIP.

Finally, David, it's very important to watch for, recognize, and celebrate when he displays leadership skills. Being a leader is very difficult, as you know. If you are going to reward your son for good grades and good games, then you should certainly reward him for good leadership. It's not important that he is the best eight-year-old leader you've ever seen, or the most polished thirteen-year-old leader out there. But what is important is that he is constantly developing his leadership skills. It's good to set the bar high and expect great things from your child, but it's equally necessary to reward his behavior and compliment his improvements.

If this all sounds difficult and overwhelming, it's because it is. Developing leadership skills in your child is tough. But that's why God gives us eighteen years with our kids. Like with the other lessons, David, don't worry about applying everything I said. I know your personality. When someone tells you to do something, you give it your all and you follow instructions down to the letter. But don't let these lessons become a burden for you. Have fun with them.

CHAPTER 20

LESSON 17: PROMOTE HEALTH CONSCIOUSNESS

THIS LESSON IS very important, David. Health has gotten so bad in our great country, and unfortunately, it's getting worse. But the crazy truth is that everyone is aware of it. I think if you asked a thousand parents if they think it's a good idea to promote a healthy lifestyle to their kids, every single one of them would say yes. But sadly, so few parents actually follow through with it.

Let me share some devastating statistics that won't surprise you. I got these from the website for the Center of Disease Control. During your lifetime, David, obesity in children has more than doubled. For teenagers, it has quadrupled. Today more than a third of children and teenagers are either overweight or obese. But weight is only a small part of the problem. Now kids are suffering from issues and diseases that used to only happen to old men like me. Children are now battling with cardiovascular issues, like high blood pressure and high cholesterol, as well as diabetes. And because of these weight and health issues, children are more depressed and have lower self-esteem than ever before. I know that you deal with this often in student ministry.

As a student minister, you may have the opportunity to help a few young people in this area. But sadly, there is very little that you can do to change society. All you can do, son, is affect your own family. I truly believe that if all parents taught their kids to be more health conscious, then many of the health issues in America would decrease drastically in one generation. But I'm aware that is very unlikely to happen. You, however, can control the lifestyle and health of your own children.

David, you must promote health consciousness to the children that God entrusts to you.

The purpose of this lesson is for you to teach Noah to have an active interest in his own health. This is way bigger than you just telling him what he can or can't eat. This is about you changing the statistics in your family. The ultimate goal is to raise a young man who understands how to live a healthy lifestyle, and who enjoys the benefits of being healthy and fit. The most effective way to accomplish this huge task is by you doing two things. First, you and Hailey must continue to live a healthy lifestyle yourselves. Second, simply explain your lifestyle to Noah as you go about life.

You know how much I enjoy working out and staying in decent shape. Many people have asked me over the years why I work out so hard, especially in my older age. I always give them the same response, David. I tell people that I work out for only three reasons. One, so that my wife will find me attractive. Two, so that I will feel good about myself. And three, so that I can be healthy enough to play with my son and set a good example to him. Now, David, you know that I am the furthest thing from a nutritional expert or fitness trainer. But my goal throughout your entire life has simply been to teach you how to become health conscious by showing you what was important to me. Then you simply copied what you saw your mother and me doing. As we did things and said things that were counterculture, we tried our best to explain why. Over time you began to understand why these health decisions were also beneficial for you.

Here are just a few things that we taught you to make you more health conscious. I pray that you will pass them on to your son.

- **Your body is a temple.** 1 Corinthians 6:19–20 says, *"Do you not know that your body is a temple of the Holy Spirit, who is in you, whom you have received from God? You are not your own; you were bought at a price. Therefore honor God with your body."*
- **Good nutrition is the foundation.** We constantly pumped you with vitamins, supplements, greens, nutrients, and vegetables.

The more organic and natural, the better. We believe that God put on the earth everything that we need to be healthy.

- **Exercise is a part of life.** Exercise is like work or church; it's just something that you do. It shouldn't be a New Year's Resolution or the way to get ready for bathing suit season. How you choose to stay in shape will vary, but exercise should be constant.

- **Playing sports is required, but being good is not.** Parents shouldn't try to live vicariously through the athletic achievements of their kids. But they should insist that their kids be active and healthy. There is no better way to achieve this than through sports. Sports force kids to run, sweat, train, and be active. It's way better than sitting on the couch playing video games. Playing sports was never an option for you, but continuing to play was. Our rule was that you had to try certain sports, and you could never quit until the season was over. But after that, we let you decide if you wanted to continue in that sport for another season.

- **Medicine is a last resort.** Don't me wrong; medicine is very important and necessary at times. You certainly had your share of medicine growing up. But don't be too quick to reach for the medicine cabinet. Do your research first. Try home remedies and natural solutions. Use essential oils and organic products. Many things can be treated without creating a dependency for medicine and pharmaceuticals.

- **Eat dinner as a family.** Make dinnertime, family time. No TV, cell phones, or electronic devices allowed. Eating dinner as a family was one of the most special times when you were growing up. It was a guaranteed opportunity every day to look one another in the eyes and talk. Not only could your mother cook something healthy, but it allowed us to slow down and enjoy being together.

- **Eat out for fun, not for convenience.** In my humble opinion families eat out way too much these days. I understand their reasoning. It's easier, faster, more convenient, and sometimes even cheaper. But it's also way unhealthier. Eating out should be something that you do occasionally for fun or to celebrate. Obviously there are exceptions to this advice. But the point is to eat at home more often than not.

- **Pray for good health.** When you were a child, I used to pray for your good health almost every day. I taught you to pray for your health as well. David, I know I'm writing this to a minister, but please remember to pray over your children. Pray for their arms and legs; pray for their lungs, heart, and brain; pray for their eyes, ears, and mouth. Always thank God for the good health that he provides.

CHAPTER 21

LESSON 18: REMEMBER WHAT'S REALLY IMPORTANT

DAVID, I CAN'T wait until baby Noah is born. Everything is about to change in your life, for the better. Being a parent is the best thing in the world. It is so much fun to watch your son grow and change each day. It is truly a blessing to see how he will turn out, what his interests will be, which gifts and abilities he has, and what type of personality he will develop. Every day is a new gift from God.

It is exciting to find out if he will like the same things that you liked as a kid. Will he be as good as you in a certain area, or even better? It's incredible to watch how his personality will spring forth from out of nowhere, and to experience his God-given gifts come out right before your eyes. I'm telling you, David, there's nothing like it in the world. Very soon he will naturally start answering questions that you don't even have to ask. Questions like:

Will he be a genius in school, or will he struggle to keep up?
Will he be the class clown, or will he be an introvert?
Will he excel in sports, or will he even make the team?
Will he love church, or will he just go because you make him?
Will he have tons of friends, or will he be more of a loner?
Will he be creative and imaginative, or will he just want to play video games?
Will he love nature and outdoors, or will he prefer technology and indoors?
Will he be popular and cool, or will he be socially awkward?

David, my guess is that even now as you are reading over these questions, your mind is already gravitating toward what you want Noah to become, and which of these answers would be hard for you to accept. Am I right? It's completely natural and normal for parents to want their kids to do, like, or become certain things. If a dad was a star baseball player back in the day, then of course he will want his son to excel in baseball or some other sport. If a mom was brilliant in school and earned an academic scholarship to college, then certainly she will want he son or daughter to be a gifted student. Personally, I have always been the life of the party and a people person, so I specifically remember hoping that you would have an outgoing and friendly personality.

Now we come to the lesson, David. As a parent, you must always remember what's really important. Yes, you must set the bar high and expect excellence from your child. Yes, you must force him at times to try new things and get outside his comfort zone. Yes, you must challenge him and push him at times to give it his all. But in doing so, please remember what is really important. Many parents live vicariously through their kids. They mean well, but their kid's accomplishments or failures can be more important to them than the child.

I know that you have experienced this in student ministry. Some parents require so much from their kids in athletics that they end up hating the very sport that they used to love. Why? Because the parents pushed too hard. Some parents are so focused on their child getting perfect grades in school that they forget about the life experiences that she is missing out on. Why? Because the parents were more concerned about her scores than the person she was becoming. David, please hear my heart. I am not trying to criticize other parents or suggest that they don't love their kids. Of course they love them, and they want what's best for them. But the problem is when parents forget what is truly important.

When you were growing up, here's what your mother and I used to tell you (and I'm sure you still remember):

- Academics: It's not important to me that you get straight As or that you are number one in your class. If you do, that's incredible. But what's important to me is that you do your very best every single day; that you study hard for every test; that you complete every assignment on time; that you pay attention in class; that you are responsible; and that you respect your teachers. If you do these things, then I will be proud of you. Good grades are important, but not nearly as important as who you are as a person.

- Athletics: It's not important to me that you are the best player on the team, that you win the game, or score twenty points, or hit a home run. If you do, I will be there to cheer you on. But what's important to me is that you work hard; that you hustle on every play; that you listen to your coach; that you have a good attitude; that you are a leader on your team; and that you have fun—after all it's just a game. If you do these things, then I will be your biggest fan.

- Friends: It's not important to me that you are the most popular kid in school, or that you have hundreds of friends. If you do, that's great. But what's important to me is that you choose quality friends; that you hang around kids who make you a better person; that you are kind and encouraging; and that you treat all people with respect. If you do these things, then you will earn my trust.

David, I hope that you understand what I am trying to teach you. I am not in any way promoting mediocrity. Noah should always strive for excellence, and that's exactly what you should demand from him. I'm simply asking you to consider that his excellence might be different from yours. He may not be able to hit a home run, but is he trying his absolute best? He may not be a natural-born leader with an outgoing personality, but is he a good boy with a moral compass? He may prefer computers over hunting and fishing, but does he love the Lord and treat people with respect? These are the types of things that really matter.

I love what the Lord says in Psalm 139:13, *"For you created my inmost being; you knit me together in my mother's womb."* Remember, David, it is God who gave your child his gifts, abilities, and personality. He literally created Noah to be unique and special. Your job as his father is simply to help him figure out how to use these to glorify God. Remember what's really important.

CHAPTER 22

LESSON 19: BE INTERESTED IN HIS INTERESTS

I WISH THAT your grandfather had lived long enough for you to know him better. He was a great man. He taught me so much about life, being a man, providing for my family, and serving the Lord. But as much as I learned from him about how to be a good father, his one great weakness is that he was never really involved in my personal life. He raised me well and he taught me many great truths, but he wasn't interested in my interests. Even as a teenager, I can clearly remember wishing that he cared more about the things that I liked. I didn't want to be like that with you, David.

I certainly had my weaknesses as a father, but I wanted so badly to be involved in your life. If there was something that peaked your interest, I wanted to know about it. I tried hard to at least act interested and make myself like it, even if I didn't always understand it. Like all kids, you went through several phases where you were absolutely obsessed with one thing. I remember buying you your first Nintendo. If we didn't make you stop to eat and sleep, you might have died playing that thing. Being raised in a military family, it was hard for me to not feel like I was wasting my time, but I made myself learn to like Mario and Tetris. Why? Because you liked it.

Then you went through a phase where you loved Pokémon cards. I thought it was the weirdest thing ever, but I sat down and played nonetheless. After a while, I started getting joy out of listening to you light up and explain these cards. I had absolutely no idea what you were talking about, but I listened and smiled. Then you went through the skateboard phase. I'm glad that didn't last long because I didn't care too much for that one. But guess what we did Saturday after Saturday? We went to the skate park together, and I watched you ride, although you spent more time on the ground than you did on the board.

I guess my favorite of all of your crazy phases is in high school when you got really into the UFC. I grew up watching boxing, so mixed martial arts was tolerable. Over time I actually started to enjoy it. The fights were exciting to watch, but the main thing was that I was with you doing what you liked. It took me many years, but I finally learned this lesson that I now want to pass on to you. Be interested in his interests.

You have shared some statistics with me in the past where adolescents say that their greatest influence in their lives is their friends. I don't believe this to be real, but if it is true, then it's certainly not because kids love their friends more than their parents. I think it's simply because their closest friends naturally share common interests. As a father, you need to be aware of this. As long as it's not something immoral or harmful, then you need to be interested in your son's interests. Make yourself like whatever it is.

Let me give you a quick side note. I am not suggesting that you constantly hover over your son and never give him any personal space or time. I am simply encouraging you to take an active interest in the people, activities, and things that are important to him. The more genuine interest you show, the more he will want you in his life. I want to share with you some things that I have found to be true. If you show an interest in his interests, then a few things will naturally happen:

1. He will be more likely to be interested in yours. Now of course, as his father you can make him do whatever you want. But the more quality time you give to the things he likes, then the more time he will give to you. I think it's fun to make trades or agreements, some good old-fashioned give and take. I'll play a video game with you, but then I want you to come with me to the driving range. Or, I will take you to the skate park tomorrow morning, but then let's watch the football game together tomorrow night.

Or, let's read your chapter book together this week, but then I get to pick the next book.

2. He will open up and trust you more. Think about it, David. His interests are where his is most comfortable and happy. This is where you will get to know him in a new light. He will let his guard down and reveal his true self. You can learn so much about your child while you are doing things that he likes. During these times he will learn to trust you more. If he learns to trust you with smaller things, then when he is older, he is more likely to trust you with more serious issues.

3. He will know that you truly care. Kids aren't stupid, David. You of all people know that. Your son will certainly know that you don't love Pokémon cards or video games. But when you give him your undivided time and attention, then he will know that you care about him. He will already know that you love him, but the jackpot is when he thinks to himself, "My dad really cares about me."

4. You can monitor his life and protect him. Ultimately your number one job as a parent is to protect your child from harm. It's easier to protect kids from the big sins like sex, drugs, and alcohol. But there are so many less obvious issues to protect kids from. When you are involved in his life at a personal level, then you will start to see what these are. For instance, you may discover that there is inappropriate language in the new music group that he likes. Or you may decide that his video games are too bloody for his age. Or you may learn that some of his friends are giving to much personal information online. These situations will provide more teachable moments, but you would have missed them if you weren't involved in his interests.

5. Finally, when you are interested in his interests, then he will want to be with you. And as long as he is with you, he is in good hands. There's nothing better than when your son truly likes being with you. It doesn't really matter what you are doing, either, as long as you two are together. Now you can protect him, mold him, teach

him, and learn more about him. A great memory just came to my mind. I remember one time when you were in high school, probably sixteen years old. It was a Saturday night and you asked me if I would order the UFC pay-per-view for you and some friends from church. I almost said no because it was fifty dollars, but I agreed. I can close my eyes and still remember that night. On a Saturday night while many teenagers were out doing bad things, my son and a dozen of his buddies were safe in my house. The coolest part is that you didn't want me to buy the fight and then leave you alone. You wanted me there with you and your friends. We even wrestled together in between the fights. That memory for me is priceless.

David, most of these lessons that I am leaving with you are about you teaching, preparing, and molding your son. They are about bringing him up to your level and making him into a godly young man. But this lesson, however, is all about you going down to his level. Allow him to be a kid. Step into his world. Experience firsthand what he likes. Just be with him. Show him that you are not only his authoritative father, but also his trusted friend.

CHAPTER 23

LESSON 20: THERE'S NO SUCH THING AS PRIVACY

I WANT TO share some statistics with you that completely hurt my heart. As a student minister, you will know these numbers all too well. There are many websites with similar numbers, but I got these from Shared Hope International.

- 42 percent of kids between seven and sixteen years old have viewed pornography online, most accidentally while doing homework.
- One in twelve have exchanged message with sexual content with another person.
- One in twenty admitted to arranging a secret meeting with someone they met online.
- 22 percent of teenage girls admitted to posting nude or semi-nude photos of themselves online.
- 65 percent of eight to fourteen year olds have been victims of cyberbullying.

David, I could go on and on with these shocking numbers. But my only purpose in writing this is to give my son some advice on how to be a great father. So let me give you one of the most important lessons that I know: There is no such thing as privacy. This has been one of my biggest soapboxes for years. Many of my more liberal friends have argued with me over this statement for years. People in our church or from work used to call me all of the time and ask my advice on parenting issues or how I would handle their child in a specific situation. I would passionately share with my friends that there should be no privacy in your house as it relates to your children. Some of them understood my meaning and applied my advice. But some thought I was an out-of-touch, controlling drill sergeant. Unfortunately, the issues with their kids never improved.

Culture, technology, and family values have changed so much in recent years. Many parents have just accepted a new reality that they no longer have any control over what their kids do. But think about it like this, David. No loving parent that I have met would ever allow: Their eleven-year-old son to view pornography online; or their thirteen-year-old daughter to be chatting online with an adult predator; or their fourteen-year-old boy to be cyberbullied; or their twelve-year-old girl to text inappropriate pictures of herself to her boyfriend. This all sounds so crazy when I say it like that. But, David, this is exactly what many parents sit back and allow their children and teenagers to do.

I am not trying to sound cynical or overly critical of other parents. But I must be honest; I have known many personal friends who indirectly hurt their own children by neglect. Now I know that parents can't control every single thing that their kid ever does. But I believe with all of my heart that there are two devastating mistakes that many parents make. One mistake is that some parents just aren't aware of what's really going on with their kids. They love them, of course, but they just don't think about their private lives. They give too much space and allow too much privacy that children and teens don't need. They actually think that their kids' phones, computers, and bedrooms are off-limits to them. I read an article just last week that said 30 percent of parents let their kids use the Internet with zero supervision or restrictions.

The second mistake that many parents make is that they care more about being friends instead of parents. They want to be peers or best buds, but the truth is that they have no backbone whatsoever. They make lousy excuses like, "Her phone is none of my business," or, "I just don't want to push him away." So instead of protecting their child, they choose to enable him. Is my passion coming through yet? I actually think my blood pressure is rising.

David, please don't be either of these. Noah needs you to protect him, even when he doesn't know it. He needs you to be is wise father, even when he doesn't ask. David, you and you alone are responsible for everything that goes on in your house and with your family. As Paul says in Ephesians 5, *"You are the head"* of your family.

To wrap up this lesson that there should be no such thing as privacy in your household, I want to give you some simple advice from one father to another:

- "Their room" is in your house. We sometimes allow descriptives like "my toys," "my clothes," or "my room." But don't forget, David, it's your house. His room is your room. I am not at all suggesting that you snoop around his room like a crazy guy. But if you have any suspicions, or if he has not been trustworthy, then you are free to look wherever you want.
- "Their cell phone" is on you bill. You may give it to him and allow him to use it, but it's ultimately your phone, too. Occasionally check his texts, social media, and especially his Internet usage. You are not being nosy; you are being wise and protective.
- No computers allowed in the bedroom. This is common sense. It amazes me how parents can read the insane statistics on children and pornography and still let their hormonal son have a computer in his room. No way! Computers must stay out in the open.
- No private passwords allowed. Don't allow him to use a password for anything, especially his cell phone and laptop. All devices are open and available for you to see.
- Lastly, teach him that social media is public and permanent. I love kids, but they can be so stupid sometimes, especially teenagers. But hey, I was the same way. Teach him that the comments he makes and the pictures he posts will stay in cyber world forever. It will affect his opportunity for a college scholarship and a job interview. But more importantly, these things can affect his witness as a Christian.

Sorry for unloading on you, David, but this lesson is very important to me. I know that you will take it seriously. The main thing is that your kids know from the beginning that there is no such thing as privacy. You need to raise them with this understanding so that there is never even a question about it. They won't know any better. You aren't suddenly shocking them with a new rule called "Dad the Dictator." You are simply raising them in a loving and protective environment. You are in charge. Kids don't demand their privacy; rather, you graciously provide it as they earn your trust and respect.

CHAPTER 24

LESSON 21: MAKE SPECIAL TIMES SPECIAL

AFTER THE LAST lesson on privacy and all of those difficult statistics, let's have some fun with this one. The next lesson is to make special times special. I learned this lesson from my parents. We didn't have much money when I was growing up. Looking back I would say that we were poor, although I didn't know it at the time. Because of dad's military duties, we were forced to move every few years, which was extremely tough on me as an only child. Every time I made a new friend, we moved. But as sad as that may sound, my childhood was great. My parents were fun and creative, and they made everything so special for me. I learned from them that creating special memories with your kids is not about money; it's about effort.

I had never really thought about this until recently, but knowing that you are going to die soon really causes you to think about things. I may be wrong about this, but I have come to the conclusion that at the end of it all, we truly only have about three things in life. We have an eternal relationship with Christ. We have the life lessons that have molded us. And we have special memories that we will take with us forever.

Think about it, son, there are so many things that seem like life or death at the time for kids and teenagers, but then they don't even last into adulthood. It's funny actually. Most childhood friends don't remain as adults. Likewise, very few childhood sweethearts actually get married. You no longer live in the same house. All of your prized possessions have been sold or given away. Your athletic career is over. Your good grades were important at the time, but no longer matter. Even that all-important first car now belongs to someone else.

These things are all great, but they take up so much of our emotion, time, money, and attention. And in the end, we take none of it with us into adulthood. I'm not trying to say that these things don't matter; clearly they do. But my point, David, is to highlight to you the importance of good memories with your family. Because special memories and these life lessons that I'm giving you will be two of the few things that Noah takes with him as an adult. So, work hard on making special times special.

As a parent it's easy to get consumed with work and life and forget about what's really important to you. Even as important as your ministry is, David, nothing is more valuable than your family, and no one needs you more than Hailey and Noah. Don't give them your leftovers; they deserve everything you've got. Give them your time, thought, and creativity. Making money is important, but money is just a tool. It's a means to an end. Making positive memories and creating special moments is simply a matter of deciding to do it.

One of the reasons that you and I have maintained such a close relationship is because we have constantly shared special moments together. They are "our memories." That's where our bond is strongest. David, you are way more creative than me and your mother put together, so it will be easy for you to come up with some special moments. But I want to give you just a few ideas to get your mind thinking and your heart focused on Noah. By the way, this particular lesson is about Noah, but you need to apply your same creative attention to that beautiful bride of yours.

This list isn't about birthdays and holidays. Those are easy to make special. This is about randomly and purposefully creating special moments and positive memories with your child. Here are a few ways to make special times special:

- Eat lunch with him at school often.
- Record everything with video or pictures.
- Leave notes under his pillow when you have to travel for work.

- Pick him up from school early and take him to a movie.
- Lay in his bed at night and just talk.
- Wake him up early and surprise him with a trip to an amusement park.
- Take him to get ice cream when you see him use his manners.
- Take him to work with you.
- At bedtime, tell him your childhood stories and memories.
- Work on a project together like building something or fixing something up.
- Go on a mission trip together as a family.
- Make up a scavenger hunt.
- Copy a famous TV game show and make up your own version at home.
- When he's young, write Santa a letter and then receive one back in the mail.
- When he gives his life to Jesus, you be the one who baptizes him.
- Take him with you to help a stranger or a family in need.
- Camp out in your backyard just for fun.
- Have a certain meal or dessert that only he helps prepare.
- Go on one-on-one dates: just father/son, or just mother/son.
- Be his coach in a sport.
- Give him a real trophy for doing something well, with his name engraved.
- Once a year, take a family trip, no other friends or relatives.
- Have a countdown calendar for a special event like a concert or trip.
- Create your own holiday traditions—for each holiday have something that you do every year; it doesn't matter how big or small it is. Just make it special and he will love it.

CHAPTER 25

LESSON 22: YOU CAN'T HUG ENOUGH

OF THE TWENTY-FIVE lessons that I am giving you, David, this one is the most obvious of them all. But remember, this final gift that I am leaving for you isn't only about learning new lessons; it's also about applying the obvious ones. This lesson is called "You can't hug enough." I think it's accurate to describe this information as something that every father knows but not every father applies. I don't know that my words here will teach you anything that you don't already know. But I do pray that they will encourage you to apply that which you do know.

Physical touch is very awkward for many men. I don't exactly understand why, but I do know that God made us very different from women. It's not that men don't like physical touch, but we just don't naturally understand how to do it in a way that is comfortable and appropriate. I have spoken to many of my male friends over the years about this because they didn't know how to use this thing called "touch" with their sons. There are three factors that I believe to be true.

Number one, men just aren't as physical as women, period. Women will joyfully hug a friend they see every week as if they have not seen each other since high school. Men don't even like to accidentally bump into other men. Number two, some men didn't receive much physical affection from their fathers, so it's hard for them to be any different with their own kids. Number three, some men actually see it as weakness or unmanly to be too affectionate with their son. Hugging and kissing might be for babies, but these fathers don't know if it's necessary for older boys.

106

These men aren't bad; they are just misinformed. I know because I was one of them. My father loved me and taught me so much about life, the Lord, and being a man. He was my hero. I wanted to be just like him in every way, except one. Physical touch wasn't his thing. My mother used to tell me that he hugged and kissed me a lot as a baby, but these actions were few and far between as I got older. I never questioned his love, but I always wondered why he didn't touch me more. In fact, his hugs were so rare that I can vividly remember one time when he did actually hug me. I was in middle school at a basketball game. I missed two free throws at the very end of the game that would have won it for our team. He met me right as I walked out of the locker room. I had tears in my eyes. He grabbed me and gave me a big bear hug. He never said a word, and neither did I. But that hug meant the world to me.

I tell you that story because I learned from my father's weakness that boys need physical touch, especially from Dad. So here is the lesson, David: hug, kiss, hold hands, cuddle, and wrestle. I can't put a price tag on the value of physical touch and why you need to apply this lesson with Noah. I have told you before that your primary goal as a father is to raise a godly young man. But don't get so caught up in trying to raise your boy into a man that you accidentally treat physical touch as childish. Touching your son daily is vital to his development both physically and emotionally. Am I basing this belief on any empirical data from well-known sociologists or psychologists? Absolutely not! It's a little thing called common sense, son.

You know me. I'm all about simple and practical. I want to give you some real life tips, David. I will not be there for you to call me later and ask me questions, so I tried to anticipate some that you may have down the road. Like most of my lessons, this is not absolute gospel truth, nor is it based on any research or recent book. It's simply my commonsense fatherly advice. And by the way, you and Hailey will probably read some parenting books that will warn you not to hold your child too much, or not to hug him when he is crying, or not to let him sleep in your bed. Also, I promise you that you will have some well-intentioned friends who think you are crazy for coddling your child or showing too much affection. David, don't worry about the opinions of others. Listen and smile, but then apply your own good judgment.

As you process it all, I want to provide you with some suggestions:

- Babies need moms more than dads in the beginning, but don't miss out of the bonding experience that takes place early in life. Hold that baby as much as you can.
- Some people say that you shouldn't hold babies when they cry so that they can learn to not always need you. But I say, you do whatever you want. I wanted you to need me. I would give anything for one more day to hold you as a baby. Don't miss the moments.
- Shower time was special for me. There obviously comes an age when it's inappropriate, but until that day comes, I say shower with him. There is something so cute about it.
- Some people will also say not to let your child sleep with you. But I say, they are only young once. Spooning with your son at night is truly one of the great joys in life. Now, David, you must keep intimacy in your marriage as a priority. I'm not suggesting that you let Noah sleep with you every night. But from time to time, it's not only OK, it's very special.
- When he gets scared at night or has a bad dream, don't send him back to bed or just say, "There's nothing to be scared of." Let him lay in bed with you for a while if he wants. He will learn to equate physical touch with security and safety.
- At bedtime, don't just walk by his room and say, "Good night." Physically tuck him in bed, hug him, and kiss him.
- Wrestle with him, throw him around, and tickle him. The more the better. Remember you are creating a strong bond with physical touch. And don't only do this when he is young, but wrestle with him as a teenager, too. He will take pride in trying to beat his dad.

- Hug him every day after school or when you get home from work. Make it the first thing you do, regardless of your stress level or mood.
- Cuddle together on the couch when watching a movie. Your mother and I used to argue over who would get to cuddle up with you on movie nights.
- When he gets good grades, don't just buy him something; embrace him with a hug.
- When he has a good game, don't just celebrate with dinner; embrace him with a hug.
- When he has a bad day, don't just try to cheer him up; embrace him with a hug.
- When he gets in trouble or spanked, after the punishment, don't just lecture him; embrace him with a hug.
- Hold hands when you are walking around. There will certainly come a day when he wants to stop holding your hand, but until then enjoy it. There is so much symbolism in a father holding his son's hand.
- At some point you will transition from kissing on the lips to kissing his cheek or forehead. That's perfectly normal, but never stop kissing him. Whether he is a baby, child, teenager, or young adult, he is still your son. Always kiss him.
- Finally, I used to say to you that hugging is not up for debate. When you got older, I compromised on some other things because I didn't want to embarrass you in public. But hugging was not one of those things. I used to say, "As long as you are my son, I'm going to hug you."
- You can't hug enough!

CHAPTER 26

LESSON 23: TEACH HIM TO THINK FOR HIMSELF

WHEN YOU WERE a kid, one of your favorite movies was *The Karate Kid*. As I'm sure you remember well, the most famous scene is when Mr. Miyagi finally reveals to young Daniel LaRusso the method to his madness. Daniel was fed up with his teacher because all he had done was make him work. Mr. Miyagi taught him to "wax on, wax off," "paint the fence" up and down, and "sand the floor" using circular motions. Hundreds of times, the teacher repeated these words and movements to his student. Finally, Daniel had enough. He wanted to learn karate, but didn't think he had learned anything so far. Before he could walk away, Mr. Miyagi proved his methods. In a very powerful scene, Mr. Miyagi attacked Daniel with punches and kicks. Without even thinking or hesitating, Daniel blocked them all using the instinctive motions that he had learned. Mr. Miyagi had taught him karate at a subconscious level. Daniel didn't have to think; he just reacted.

Many of the lessons that I am giving you are just like this. The goal is to teach Noah certain things at a subconscious level using strategy, love, and repetition. You want him to learn these lessons at his core so that he doesn't even had to think about them; he just reacts. For example, if you instill in him the value of manners, gratitude, and self-discipline, then Lord willing, these will become a part of his lifestyle without even thinking about them. But this lesson, David, is the exact opposite. This isn't about teaching him at a subconscious level; rather, for this lesson you must be direct with your approach. Your strategy is to be upfront and to the point. Tell him often, "My goal is to teach you how to think for yourself and make wise decisions."

Proverbs 23:7 says, *"As a man thinks in his heart, so is he."* I love this verse because Solomon reminds us of the power of the mind. Whatever we think about the most, we bring about in reality. But here is the problem, David. And I hope that I am able to explain myself well. Sometimes I know what I mean in my heart, but it's difficult to express with words. Schools and churches are great at teaching kids *what* to think, or what is *true*. While this information that's taught is extremely valuable and necessary, I believe it's still incomplete. As a father, you must go a step further and teach your son *how* to think and what is *wise*.

Here is another fact to consider. Think for a moment about the mass information that kids take in each day. They play video games, watch YouTube, spend time on Facebook, and get caught up in reality TV or kids shows. None of these are bad, David. I'm not trying to sound like an old, out-of-touch man. But please hear my heart. All of these examples are completely void of requiring kids to think for themselves. Kids can get lost in cyberspace or TV land for hours a day if you let them. I'm simply trying my best to make the case that that few people will ever teach Noah *how* to think for himself. But that's OK because God gave him a great father.

I want to help you with this difficult, but important task, David. I want to share with you some insights that I have learned through the years. Most of these I have used with you throughout your lifetime. A few of these I learned from other wise men who have mentored me. Teach Noah information and you can make him smart, but teach him how to think and you can make him wise. These are strategies that you can apply as a father in order to teach your son how to think for himself.

1) GIVE HIM CHOICES.

As a father I think it's often beneficial to remember what it's like to be a kid. For the most part, kids don't have many choices. They simply do what they are told, which is exactly how it should be. But in order to get him thinking, you must first give him choices. I don't mean choices like, "Do you want Captain Crunch or Lucky Charms?" I mean give him choices that matter. When he is young, these choices will be more juvenile, but as he gets older, allow them to become more vital. For example, when young Noah asks for a sucker when you go through to the bank. Instead of just saying no, you could let him choose. "Remember we are having birthday cake tonight. I don't want you having too much sugar, so you can't have both. I think you shouldn't eat the sucker, but I will let you choose. Do you want the sucker now, or a big plate of cake later?" Here's another example as he gets older. "I know that the youth group has two trips coming up, but we can't afford to do both. But we will let you choose. Do you want to go on the ski trip, or to the Disciple Now Weekend?"

2) TEACH HIM TO WEIGH THE PROS AND CONS.
This was one of the most valuable lessons that I ever taught you. When you were seven years old, you wanted to use your own money to buy a certain video game. This wasn't about instant gratification; in fact, you wanted this game for months. It was going to cost you all of your money that you had saved for several months. I remember sitting you down with a piece of paper and drawing a line down the middle from top to bottom. On one column I wrote pros, and on the other I wrote cons. I explained how important it is to weigh the pros and cons before we make an important decision in any area of life. I said before I decide what I will let you do, you must first write down every pro and con for buying this expensive game. I made you take your time and really think about it, and said that we wouldn't discuss it until the next day because I didn't want you to make the decision on emotion. The next day you presented me with a well-thought-out list. I was so proud of you, so I let you buy the game. From that time on, you used the pros and cons system to help yourself make big decisions.

3) BE VERY CLEAR ABOUT YOUR RULES AND THE CONSEQUENCES.
To help your son be able to think for himself, you need to clearly communicate your rules, as well as the consequences for breaking them.

112

When he does break a rule, even if it is small, how you handle it can literally teach him how to think. Don't just punish him, but teach him also. I used to ask you the same questions each time you broke a rule. I said, "Did you know that this was wrong?" Then I let you answer. I said, "Did I explain what would happen if you did this?" Then I let you answer. I said, "If you knew both of these things, then who decided to do it anyway?"

You would answer, "I did, Daddy." It's not just about punishment or discipline, but it's also about teaching him how to think and reason, even at a young age. But the rules and consequences must be very clear up front.

4) MAKE HIM EXPLAIN THE EXACT REASON THAT HE IS IN TROUBLE, OR WHAT HE DID WRONG.

When your child does something wrong or bad, it's very easy to go straight into parent mode and give him a lecture. I made this mistake often when you were young until one day I realized that half the time you didn't truly understand why you were in trouble. So I learned to ask questions and listen. And I kept asking questions until you thought clearly about the situation and gave the right answers. For example, let's say I spanked you and sent you to your room. I would come in after a while and the first thing I would ask is, "Why are you in here?"

If you said something like, "Because I'm in trouble," or, "Because you told me to," then I would say, "Think about why you are in here and then yell for me when you're ready to talk." Then I left. After doing this a few times, it forced you to think about the true reason, admit your mistakes, and apologize. It's easy for parents to give answers too quickly, but it's better to force kids to think about it for themselves.

5) TEACH HIM TO ASK: WHAT IS THE WISE THING TO DO (BEFORE MAKING THE DECISION)?

This is my favorite question to ask in my personal life when I am faced with any decision, large or small. I taught you this question, and I hope that you pass it on. At the root of this lesson on teaching your child how to think is the word *wisdom*. Please teach Noah the difference between smart and wise. Teach him how and why to ask the question, "What is the wise thing to do?" The reason it's so valuable is because there are many situations in life that are not about good and bad or right and wrong. I tell adults all of the time that there is nothing sinful about a married man having lunch alone with a married coworker. It's not wrong, but it is very unwise. Teach Noah to think in terms of wisdom. Before he makes a tough decision, he should ask: What is the wise thing to do?

6) ASK HOW HE COULD HAVE HANDLED THE SITUATION BETTER (AFTER THE DECISION).

What about after he has made a decision that wasn't wise? Remember, in these situations your child didn't break a rule and he doesn't deserve a punishment. He simply handled a situation poorly, or made an unwise decision that he regrets. Now is the time to help him learn how to make better decisions in the future. Again, instead of telling him what you would have done, it's better to start by asking questions. Ask, "Now that you have had time to think about it, how could you have handled the situation better?" And then listen. Don't interrupt or complete his sentences; just listen.

7) TEACH USING SCENARIOS.

Scenarios are a great way to get kids and teenagers thinking. Have fun with this one. Give him random scenarios when you are in the car, at the dinner table, getting ready for bed, or whenever. Make some of them playful, but at times it's also good to make them serious and realistic. This isn't about goofy conversations but instead teaching him how to think. Scenarios are great because you can learn where his heart is on certain issues. My personal favorite scenarios start with either: "What would you do if..." or, "How would you handle..." For example, "Noah, what would you do if you were at your friend's house and he was watching a movie with bad language?" Or, "If you were at school and some mean kids were picking on another kid, how would you handle it?" Try to think of realistic scenarios that he could or will likely face. Most kids don't think; they just react when they find themselves in a difficult situation. But when you can get him thinking about certain real-life scenarios, then you are literally preparing him ahead of time to be ready.

8) TEACH HIM TO NEGOTIATE.
Nothing can get our minds thinking quite like negotiating. I think it's very important to teach this skill to kids. It forces them to be prepared, to think ahead, to counter-offer, and to know when to walk away. First teach Noah what it means to negotiate, and then give him opportunities to grow. Make deals with him, make trades, make him offers, let him win some, and let him lose some. Negotiating is an important part of life and business. Teach him young and prepare him to think.

9) OCCASIONALLY ALLOW HIM TO MAKE THE WRONG CHOICE, AND THEN THOROUGHLY DISCUSS THE OUTCOME.
One of the hardest things to do as parents is to willfully allow your kids to make bad decisions. We know what the outcome will be, but sometimes we have to let them learn the hard way. Assuming that it won't harm your child physically or morally, I encourage you to sometimes let him make wrong choices. When this occurs, how you handle it will often determine what he learns from it. Don't rub it in his face and don't say, "I told you so." But also don't miss the teachable moment. Thoroughly discuss the outcome, his feelings, his regrets, and most importantly, how he can learn and grow from it.

10) EXPLAIN HOW AND WHY YOU MAKE CERTAIN DECISIONS IN YOUR LIFE.
There is no better teacher than life itself. When you have a big decision to make in your life, tell him about it. He will feel so honored that you

are being open and vulnerable. Explain to him how you make decisions, or why you are torn in a given situation. He will learn so much about the process of decision-making just from watching you and hearing your explanation.

11) ALLOW HIM TO HELP YOU SOLVE MINOR PROBLEMS OR ISSUES.

If you really want to make your son feel special, allow him to help you solve problems or make decisions. It doesn't matter how big or small the issue is, just let him help. Say things like, "OK buddy, I need your advice. Can you help me weigh the pros and cons?" Or, "Let's figure this out together." Or, "What do you think I should do?" Or, "Here's what I decided. Do you agree or disagree?"

12) PRAY WITH HIM FOR WISDOM AND DISCERNMENT.

My mother taught me this lesson when I was a teenager. I had spent years asking God for things, but it had never occurred to me to ask for wisdom. Since then I have continuously asked God for wisdom and discernment. My advice to you, David, is to pray with Noah and consistently ask God to fill him with wisdom and discernment. Teach Noah that wisdom comes from God, and that seeking wisdom is a lifelong journey. 2 Chronicles 1: 7–10 says, *"That night God appeared to Solomon and said to him, 'Ask for whatever you want me to give you.' Solomon said, 'Give me wisdom and knowledge, that I may lead this people, for who is able to govern this great people of your?'"*

13) REMIND HIM OFTEN THAT YOUR GOAL IS TO TEACH HIM HOW TO THINK FOR HIMSELF.

I will end this lesson where we started. In order to teach your son how to think for himself, you must be direct. I used to tell you all of the time, "David, my goal is to teach you how to think for yourself, and I only have eighteen years to achieve it." Sometimes you thought I was funny, and other times annoying, but you always understood that I was focused on your development. Be honest with Noah. Tell him what you are doing and explain why you do so many things that other parents don't do. And always remind him that you won't stop until you teach him to think for himself.

CHAPTER 27

LESSON 24: RAISE YOUNG MEN, NOT OLD BOYS

DAVID, I'M FEELING very weak and sick today. My mind isn't very clear, so I'm praying that I will be able to articulate what's in my heart. You above all people know that I am normally a positive and optimistic person. But I must be vulnerable and honest with you. I feel like I owe you that. David, I honestly don't know how much longer I have. I have been asking God to give me enough time to finish this gift for you and to be able to give it to you myself. I am thankful for the strength and mental clarity to have been able to write down twenty-three lessons so far. But my gift is incomplete without the final two lessons, so I will give you my all.

This lesson is very important to me. Your mother and I have several friends in our Sunday school class who have grown children in their twenties and thirties, but they still haven't grown up. Our friends are frustrated and concerned. They are wondering what they did wrong, or what they could have done differently to raise them better into maturity. Their grown kids are not bad people at all, but they are old boys and girls, and not yet young men and women. My heart hurts for my friends, but my greater concern is you, Hailey, and Noah.

As I've said many times now, the overall goal of any Christian parent should be to raise their child into a godly young man or woman. The "godly" part is easy for you to understand and apply. I have already given you the lesson on laying a strong biblical foundation, so I'm not going to spend any more time on that. Plus, I know that you will raise Noah according to the instructions of God's Holy Word. But in this lesson I want to focus on what it means to raise a young man.

There are too many old boys in our society today, and not enough young men. This has nothing to do with age, either. I know plenty of forty-year-old boys and twenty-five-year-old men. Raising a young man is more about who he is as a person and how he chooses to live his life. But let me be clear about one thing. When Noah is a child, allow him to be a child. When he is a teenager, let him be a teenager. You are not trying to strip him of his childhood and force him to be like you. You are raising a young man, but you must do so in a way that is natural. Your job is to teach him and raise him with the end in mind. Some parents literally watch their kids walk across the graduation stage and simply hope that they turn our well. But you and Hailey should raise Noah in such a way that you expect him to be a certain way, act a certain way, and live a certain way.

Proverbs 22:6 is one verse that I encourage you to memorize. It was a mantra for me when you were little. It says, *"Train a child in the way he should go, and when he is old he will not turn from it."* There is no guarantee that Noah will not one day get off the path that God has for him, the path that you have raised him on. But I do promise you, David, that if you raise him using these lessons that I am giving you, then he will eventually return to that path. I've thought long and hard about exactly what I want to say in this lesson. It's much easier to teach this lesson in person as you go through life than it is to write it down. But you and I won't have that luxury, so here's what I want to share with you. I want to give you some real-life examples of what an old boy looks likes in my opinion, and then paint a picture of what a godly young man looks like.

First, here are some examples of what I think an old boy looks like. An old boy is a person who is the age of a man, but he lives and acts more like a boy. He may even have a family and a career, but he is more into himself than his family. This doesn't mean that he is a bad guy; he just has some growing up to do. This person is a grown adult male, but he is not a man in my book.

- He spends too much time playing video games or fantasy sports. There is nothing wrong with doing either of these, but for this guy it's way too important and time consuming.
- He lives with his parents way too long.
- He spends money that he doesn't have using credit cards. He lives for the moment and racks up a lot of consumer debt.
- He changes jobs every couple of years. He knows nothing of loyalty. He is looking to jump ship every time another offer is available.
- He blames his boss, the economy, or anyone else instead of taking personal accountability for his decisions.
- He willingly stabs people in the back in order to climb the corporate ladder.
- He refuses to tithe to his church because finances are too tight, but he spends thousands of dollars on golf, hunting, or his favorite sports team.
- He doesn't have time to spend with God, but he has plenty of time for drinks after work with his buddies.

David, this description of an old boy may sound harsh, but it's a reality for many people that I know. The descriptions I just gave you are all literal examples from families in my church. I know that you also have several friends that you went to school with who still haven't really grown up yet. But Noah will not look like this. And how do I know? Because you are beginning with the end in mind. When you know what the end result should look like, then you can take steps to accomplish that goal. You can start molding your son and instilling these traits in him. In my humble opinion, here is the end. This is what a godly young man looks like.

- He is humble—He doesn't think to highly of himself.
- He is mature—He sets aside his boyish behavior and decides to live with maturity and responsibility.

- He is accountable—He takes personal accountability for his life. He doesn't blame others. He knows that he is where he is in life because of his own choices.
- He is wise—He echoes the prayer of Solomon and asks God daily for wisdom and discernment.
- He is driven—He works hard, sets goals, and stops at nothing to achieve them.
- He is giving—He not only tithes to his church, but he willingly gives to people in need. He has a heart to help and support others.
- He is kind—He loves people and treats them with respect.
- He is a good steward—He saves a portion of his income, lives below his means, and doesn't spend money that he doesn't have on credit cards.
- He is respected—He has a good name and reputation in his community as a person of character and integrity. Proverbs 22:1 says, *"A good name is more desirable than great riches."*
- He is grounded—He knows what he believes and why he believes it. His faith is not shaken by the ever-changing culture. Romans 12:2 says, *"Do not conform to the patterns of this world, but be transformed by the renewing of your mind."*

This, David, is what a godly young man looks like. But these are just words. If you want to visually see this list of qualities manifested in a person, then just look in the mirror. When I made this list, I simply thought of you and the kind of man that you are. Noah will be this kind of young man, too, one day because he will spend his whole life looking up to you.

CHAPTER 28

LESSON 25: PRAY CONSISTENTLY

DAVID, I SAVED this lesson for last on purpose. None of the other lessons are in any order whatsoever, except for the first two and this last one. I wanted to start by sharing with you just how important your role is as a father. Then I shared the value of creating a biblical foundation in your family. Finally, I chose to end with the power of prayer.

Here's the truth. Almost every one of the lessons that I've given you can be learned and taught based on your personal effort, desire, and passion. *You* can teach him self-discipline. *You* can teach him manners. *You* can fill his mind with success mottos. *You* can teach him money lessons. It's all simply a matter of you deciding that you want to be a great father and then doing something about it. But here is an undeniable truth that I have learned over and over as a father for the last thirty-one years. You can't do it all on your own. Why would you even want to try?

In Matthew 7:9–11 Jesus says, *"Which of you, if his son asks for bread, will give him a stone? Or, if he asks for a fish, will give him a snake? If you, then, though you are evil, know how to give good gifts to your children, how much more will your Father in heaven give good gifts to those who ask him!"*

You will be a great father, David, whether I am around to help you or not. I know this because you will rely on the power of your Heavenly Father. And by the way, every one of my lessons came straight from God's Word. They are not my own. I know nothing except that which my Father has given me. But don't miss the key to this passage. You ask me often how I seem to know how to handle situations, or how do I give such good advice, or how did I become so wise. Well, son, here it is: I have much because I ask much. In verse 11 of Matthew 7, it says, *"How much more will your Father give good gifts to those who ask him!"* So the real question is what do I ask for? The short answer is wisdom and discernment to be able to raise my son according to God's Word.

David, please allow this old, dying man to give you one final admonition. Your greatest role as a Christian father is to be an intercessor. As you know, an intercessor is a person who intervenes and goes to God on behalf of another person. There is no better way to serve your son then by bathing him in prayer, or by interceding for him in prayer. I want to give you one final verse that has guided my life as a father more than any other.

1 Samuel 12:23 says, *"As for me, far be it from me that I should sin against the Lord by failing to pray for you. And I will teach you the way that is good and right."* David, please make this covenant with the Lord that you will not commit the *"sin of failing to pray"* for Noah as you teach him *"the way that is good and right."* Be his intercessor.

Pray for him consistently, David. Pray for his salvation. Pray for his future wife. Pray for him to pick good friends. Pray for his health and safety. Pray for his personality. Pray for him to have a kind spirit. Pray that he would overcome temptations. Pray for the armor of God to protect him against the enemy. And certainly pray for personal wisdom and discernment to know how to raise him well.

But don't just pray for him; also pray with him. Teach him how to pray and what to pray for. Allow him to hear you pray. There is nothing better for a child than hearing his father talk to the Father. And finally, pray over him. Go into his room when he is asleep, lay your hands on him, and pray fervently.

CHAPTER 29

THE LAST PAGE

DAVID, I WANT to share some final thoughts with you. As I'm writing this it's almost midnight on Sunday night. I couldn't sleep so I decided to get up and write this last page. I'm feeling pretty awful right now. I was going to wait and finish this in the morning, but I felt prompted to do it tonight. You know those times when you feel like you are supposed to do something but you don't really know why? I tell ya, son, I think I overexerted myself today working in the garage. Everyone keeps telling me to slow down, but I can't just lie down and give up. But the truth is my body is certainly getting weaker each day.

I have the worst headache right now that I've ever had. This brain cancer has given me some intense migraines, but nothing like this. And for some reason, my nose won't stop bleeding. If you could see me right now, you would laugh. I have a cold, wet towel over my head and tissue paper jammed up both nostrils to stop the bleeding. I'm a hot mess, son. My eyes are full of tears, but my heart is full of joy. I'm a blessed man. I also wrote your mother a letter today. I'm not sure how to give it to her or when. Maybe I will need your help on that one.

Even though my head hurts and my mind is foggy, I'm feeling inspired to finish this last page because of our phone call earlier tonight. By the way, if I have never told before, our Sunday night call is the highlight of my week. Thank you for taking the time each week for this old man. You asked me tonight if I was scared when you were born. Then you said that you are scared and nervous about being a father. You had an uncomfortable tone to your voice that I've never heard. I was sad that our conversation got cut short, but that's where we left it. I have to admit something.

When you told me that you were nervous about Noah being born in four weeks, I didn't say anything, but I was smiling on my end of the phone. I'm certainly not happy that you are scared. But it made me even more excited to give you this gift.

I have been writing these lessons now for over five months. I want you to know that I have almost stopped several times. The enemy keeps planting seeds of doubt and inadequacy in my mind. He keeps saying, "Who you are, Tom, that you should give parenting advice to anyone?"

But then there's that still small voice in my heart that says, "These are not your words, Tom. They are mine. I gave these lessons to you, and I want you to pass them on." I have chosen to listen to the second voice because I know him well. So my prayer, David, is that these lessons will add value to you as a father, as they have for me. And now I want to finish by suggesting how to best implement these lessons in your life.

You have heard the expression that knowledge is power. While this is true, I think it's incomplete. Knowledge is simply the potential for power. It's what you decide to do with knowledge that makes a lasting difference in your life and in the lives of others. Here's my point: Don't just read over these lessons and then put them back in the box. I gave them to you to use, implement, and share. So this is literally my final advice to you, son. Set aside a specific time each week for these lessons. I was thinking maybe Sunday nights at 8:00 p.m. Each week read over one lesson at a time, only one per week. By the end of the year, you will have read each lesson two times.

But please do more than just read them. I want them transfer from your head to your heart. Get a journal and start taking notes. As you read over each lesson, insert your own thoughts and ideas. Think about creative and practical ways to implement each one. Ask yourself, "How can I grow in this area?" Or, "How can I apply this lesson immediately?" Or maybe even, "Is this lesson relevant in my life right now?" Each time that you read the lessons, they will likely speak to you differently, especially as you get older and wiser.

Finally, here is the key, David. If you truly want to build a great family legacy, and I know you do; then go over each lesson with Hailey. Get on the same page with your wife. Decide together how you two can best raise your son. God not only called you to be a father, but he also called her to be a mother. The husband is to be the head of the household, but the head can't survive without the body. Implement these lessons together. This is my final gift to you.

David, I am usually good with words, but I have absolutely no idea how to end this letter. How do I say good-bye to my only son? For the last few months as I've been writing this, my plan has been to give it to you when Noah is born, along with a box of other special items. But I don't think that's going to happen. I have been asking God for the opportunity, but he may have different plans. So here is what I want you to know. Being married to your mother and being your father have been the two greatest blessings of my life. I didn't deserve you two, but God, in his infinite mercy, chose to bless me. And now I think that my Heavenly Father is ready for me. So probably for the final time, I want you to know:

You are special.

God loves you.

And Daddy loves you, David.

CHAPTER 30

THE FIRST PAGE

DAVID CLOSED THE notebook and sat motionless. He was in complete shock.

"Dad literally died less than three hours after he finished writing," David thought to himself. "Did he somehow know that he was dying?"

Out of the corner of his eye, David saw a ray of sunlight coming through the window. He had been up reading all night. He was physically and emotionally exhausted. He had cried so much that he truly had no more tears left to give. But for some reason, the sunshine was invigorating, as it lit up the dark room. David felt a sudden sense of warmth in his body. For the first time all night, a smirk appeared on his face. He wasn't crying, and he wasn't sad; he was proud.

David slowly began putting everything back in the box carefully as if he were packing expensive China dishes. First he grabbed for the journals and stared at them. "I need to buy one of these," he thought to himself as he set them in the box. Next he put back his old Bible that his dad had engraved Noah's name on. Then he stacked up all of the Success Motto cards and placed them in the box gently. He was careful not to bend the edges. After that he reached for his favorite childhood picture and briefly starred at him and his father.

"Thank you for this amazing gift, Dad," he said out loud, as if talking to the picture.

The notebook was still in his lap where it had been all night. As he picked it up to put in back in the box, a small half sheet of white paper fell out the bottom of the notebook. It had been tucked in between the last sheet of paper and the back of the notebook. As he reached down to pick it up, he saw that it was a handwritten note. David instantly recognized the handwriting. It was the same large cursive letters that he had seen thousands of times growing up on every letter, birthday card, and Christmas present. The note was from his mother.

My Sweet David,

I want to start by saying that I debated as to whether or not I should write you this note. In no way do I want to take anything away from your father's great lessons. He has worked so hard to give you everything that he wants you to have before he passes. I wish you only knew how important this project has been for him, and how excited he is to pass down these parenting lessons to you. To be honest, I think it has kept him alive. But call it a mother's intuition. I just felt led to share one thing with you. 1 Corinthians 15:10 has been a theme verse for my life. It says, "But by the grace of God I am what I am, and his grace toward me was not in vain."

I know how much you look up to your father. He is your hero. But please, David, as you read through his lessons, remember one thing: grace. Your father is the best man I know. He is an amazing husband and an even better father. But he is not perfect. He is a sinner just like everyone else. God's grace and mercy has been poured out in his life and in mine. Please hear my heart, my precious boy. As you read his words and apply his advice, do so knowing that you will not be a perfect father, either. You will have times when you do everything wrong, when you mess up, and when make poor decisions. In those times, please recall the inspiring words of Paul. "But by the grace of God I am what I am."

For some undeserved reason, God has chosen to bless our family with his grace, mercy, and love. And just as He will bestow his grace on you when you fail as a father, extend the same amount of grace to Noah when he fails as a son. It's all about grace, David. I love you and I am so proud of you.

Mom

David smiled as he tucked his mother's note back in the notebook. His mother always knew what to say to make him feel good. Her words were perfect. He set the notebook back in the box and closed the lid. Then David did the only thing that he could think of. He got down on his knees.

"God, I love you so much," David prayed aloud. "Thank you for blessing me such amazing parents. Thank you for a mother who gives me proper perspective. When I feel like I have to try to be perfect, she reminds me of your amazing grace, Lord. Thank you for a father who has spent his life preparing me for mine. Thank you for giving me thirty-one years to be with him and learn from him. And thank you for taking him home before he suffered even more. Holy Spirit, I need you. I want to become a great father for Noah. Please fill me with your wisdom and discernment. Help me, Lord, to raise him according to your Holy Word. Father, allow me to learn from my dad's lessons and use them to raise Noah into a godly young man. I give Noah to you because he is yours. Give me the faith of Abraham when he was willing to sacrifice his son Isaac. God, I trust that you will show me what to do. Help me to lead my family with honor. Jesus, I love you, and I thank you that you first loved me."

Two days later, David and Hailey were back home in Louisville. It was Sunday, but David had already requested the day off, so they stayed home from church.

"It feels weird not being in church on Sunday morning," David said as he was making a pot of coffee.

"You needed it, honey," Hailey responded while giving him a good-morning hug. "I know that you're tough, but you're not Superman. You need to rest and recharge your batteries."

"I agree," David replied as he gave her a kiss on the head. "But I do need to run to the store today, so if we need anything while I'm there, let me know."

"Actually we need several things," Hailey said quickly without skipping a beat. As she started to list them off, David interrupted with a laugh.

"Baby, what are you doing?" David joked. "How long have we been married? You know that I won't remember anything you're saying. Write down a list and I'll take care of it."

Hailey smiled and agreed. "I don't know what I was thinking. If I don't make a list, you will only come home with chocolate ice cream and grilled chicken."

David laughed because she knew him all too well.

"What else could we possibly need?" David said as he walked out of the room to go get dressed.

At 8:00 p.m. an alarm went off on David's cell phone that he had set as a reminder. He turned off the football game, grabbed his phone, and walked upstairs to his office. As he pushed the button to silence the alarm, he thought about his dad. This was the first time in several years that his dad hadn't called him at 8:00 p.m. Before he went to his office, he first walked into his bedroom. Hailey was lying on the bed, reading a book.

"Hey, baby, do you need anything?" David asked.

"Actually, yes, can you please bring me some water?" Hailey answered.

When David returned with the water, he leaned down and gave her a long kiss on the lips.

"How are you feeling?" he asked.

"I'm feeling fat!" she quickly replied with a smile.

David immediately responded, "You are phat with a 'ph,' baby!" It wasn't funny but Hailey giggled anyway.

"You're a dork!" she said. "By the way, how are you holding up tonight?" Hailey asked with concern. She knew that this was normally the time when David talked on the phone to his dad.

"I think I'm fine. Thanks for asking," David said as he started walking out of the room. "I'm going to my office to read a little. If you need me, just yell."

"OK honey, I love you," Hailey said. She knew her husband well enough to know when he was hurting.

"I love you, too!" David said.

David sat down at his desk and opened the box. Just like before, he was very careful with everything he handled. He took out the black notebook on the bottom and opened up to lesson one. Then he grabbed a pen and a notepad. David decided to take his father's final advice and read over one lesson each week. He chose carryout this discipline every Sunday night at 8:00 p.m. Pen in hand, ready to take notes and write down his thoughts, he began reading lesson one.

"Fathers Are So Important..."

Thirty minutes later, David closed his father's notebook and set down his pen. His notepad was full of notes, questions, Bible verses, thoughts, and ideas. David smiled. He felt alive and confident.

"I am important and Noah needs me," he thought.

Then he set down the notepad and reached for the brand-new journal that he had bought earlier that day. David touched it to his nose and took a deep whiff. He loved the smell of leather. With a huge grin on his face, David opened the journal, put the date at the top, and then began entry number one.

"Dear Noah, you are three weeks from being born. Your mommy and I can't wait to meet you. I think you are also excited to see us too because you kick and punch every day, trying to get out. I wanted to take a minute to tell you what's going on. This has been a very hard week for me. My daddy passed away a few days ago. He was my very close friend and mentor. My heart is sad because you will never get to meet your papa. That's what he wanted you to call him. Your papa was the best man I know and an incredible father. But don't you worry, buddy, because he taught me everything I need to know to be a great father for you. Right here and now I want to make a covenant between you, God, and me. I promise that I will do my best raise you according to God's Word. I will not be perfect, but when I mess

up, I will own it and ask for forgiveness. My goal is to raise you to become a godly young man one day. You have my word. And finally, there are three things that I want you to know for sure:

> *#1 You are special!*
> *#2 God loves you!*
> *#3 Daddy loves you!*

Daddy